WEIGHT WATCHERS®

STIR-FRY TO SZECHUAN
100 Classic Chinese Recipes

Macmillan • USA

MACMILLAN

A Simon & Schuster Macmillan Company
1633 Broadway
New York, NY 10019

Text copyright ©1997 Weight Watchers, International, Inc.

A Word about Weight Watchers

Since 1963, Weight Watchers has grown from a handful of people to millions of enrollments annually. Today, Weight Watchers is recognized as the leading name in safe and sensible weight control. Weight Watchers members form a diverse group, from youths to senior citizens, attending meetings virtually around the globe.

Weight-loss and weight-management results vary by individual, but we recommend that you attend Weight Watchers meetings, follow the Weight Watchers food plan and participate in regular physical activity. For the Weight Watchers meeting nearest you, call 1-800-651-6000.

Weight Watchers Publishing Group

Editorial Director: Nancy Gagliardi
Senior Editor: Martha Schueneman
Food and Nutrition Editor: Regina Regone, M.S., R.D.
Editorial Assistant: Christine Senft, M.S.
Recipe Developers: Sandra Rose Gluck and Joyce Hendley, M.S.
Nutrition Consultants: Lynne S. Hill, M.S., R.D., L.D. and William Hill, M.S., R.D., L.D.
Photographer: David Bishop
Food Stylist: Mariann Sauvion

Library of Congress Cataloging-in-Publication Data
Stir-fry to Szechuan: 100 classic Chinese recipes / Weight Watchers.
    p.   cm.
    Includes index
    ISBN 0-02-861718-5
    1. Reducing diets—Recipes. 2. Cookers, Chinese. I. Weight Watchers International.
RM222.2.S843   1997
641.5'635—dc21   97-4298
                                CIP

Manufactured in the United States of America

10 9 8 7 6 5 4 3 2

Interior Design by Rachael McBrearty

table of
CONTENTS

Hot-and-Sour Soup with Mushrooms

makes 4 servings

This popular Chinese soup gets its fiery kick from ginger, hot red pepper sauce and black pepper.

10 dried Chinese black mushroom caps*
    (about 1 ounce)

1 tablespoon cornstarch

1 tablespoon reduced-sodium soy sauce

1 tablespoon rice wine or dry sherry

½ teaspoon sugar

5 ounces sirloin tip, cut into ¼" strips

2 teaspoons Asian sesame oil

2 cups sliced shiitake mushrooms

2 cups sliced oyster mushrooms

16 scallions, minced

4 cups low-sodium chicken broth

3 tablespoons rice vinegar

1 teaspoon ground ginger

½ teaspoon hot red pepper sauce

¼ teaspoon freshly ground black pepper

2 small sweet potatoes, peeled and cut
    into 1" chunks

½ pound firm reduced-fat tofu, cut into
    1" chunks

1. In a small saucepan, bring 2 cups water to a boil. Add the black mushrooms; cover and remove from heat. Let stand until softened, about 20 minutes. Drain, reserving the liquid, and thickly slice the mushrooms. Strain the soaking liquid through a cheesecloth-lined strainer.

2. Meanwhile, in a small bowl, combine the cornstarch, soy sauce, wine and sugar. Add the beef and toss to coat.

3. In a large nonstick saucepan, heat the oil until it just begins to smoke, 30–40 seconds. Add the shiitake and oyster mushrooms and the scallions; cook, stirring as needed, until the mushrooms have released and then reabsorbed their liquid.

4. Stir in the broth, vinegar, ginger, pepper sauce, pepper, the black mushrooms and the soaking liquid; bring to a boil. Add the sweet potatoes; reduce the heat and simmer, covered, until the potatoes are tender and the flavors are blended, about 15 minutes. Return to a boil and add the beef mixture and tofu; cook, stirring constantly, until the beef is just cooked through and the soup is slightly thickened, about 1 minute.

spicy

Serving provides:
1 Bread, 2 Fruit/
Vegetables, 2
Protein/Milks, 1 Fat.

Per serving:
241 Calories,
8 g Total Fat,
2 g Saturated Fat,
22 mg Cholesterol,
367 mg Sodium,
30 g Total
Carbohydrate,
5 g Dietary Fiber,
18 g Protein, 83 mg
Calcium.

Points per serving: 4.

*See Glossary, page 133.

Spicy Pork Soup with Cellophane Noodles

makes 4 servings

Peanut oil adds a traditionally Chinese flavor to this soup. It also has a very high smoking point, so it's ideal for stir-frying and sautéing over high heat.

1 tablespoon + 2 teaspoons cornstarch

10 ounces trimmed lean pork loin, cut into ¼" strips

1 tablespoon + 1 teaspoon peanut oil

16 scallions, thinly sliced

3 tablespoons minced peeled gingerroot

5 garlic cloves, minced

5 cups low-sodium chicken broth

1 tomato, chopped

1 tablespoon reduced-sodium soy sauce

1 tablespoon rice vinegar

¾ teaspoon hot chili paste*

3 ounces cellophane noodles,* broken into 6" lengths

¾ cup sliced water chestnuts

½ cup minced cilantro

1. Place 1 tablespoon of the cornstarch in a plastic bag; add the pork and shake to coat.

2. In a medium, heavy saucepan, heat 1 tablespoon of the oil until it just begins to smoke, 30–40 seconds. Reduce the heat and add the pork; cook, stirring as needed, until lightly browned, about 3 minutes. With a slotted spoon, transfer to a plate.

3. In the same saucepan, heat the remaining 1 teaspoon of the oil. Add the scallions, ginger and garlic; cook, stirring constantly, until the scallions begin to soften, about 1 minute. Stir in the broth, tomato, soy sauce, vinegar and chili paste; bring to a boil. Reduce the heat and simmer, covered, until the flavors are blended, about 5 minutes.

4. Meanwhile, place the cellophane noodles in a medium bowl with enough hot water to cover. Let stand until softened, about 10 minutes. Drain and add the noodles to the soup, along with the pork, water chestnuts and cilantro; return to a boil.

5. In a small bowl, stir the remaining 2 teaspoons of the cornstarch into 1 tablespoon water; stir into the soup and cook, stirring constantly, until slightly thickened, about 1 minute.

See Glossary, page 133.

one pot

spicy

Serving provides:
1 Bread, 1 Fruit/ Vegetable, 2 Protein/ Milks, 1 Fat.

Per serving:
313 Calories,
12 g Total Fat,
3 g Saturated Fat,
42 mg Cholesterol,
371 mg Sodium,
35 g Total Carbohydrate,
2 g Dietary Fiber,
21 g Protein,
73 mg Calcium.

Points per serving: 7.

Vegetable Soup with Meatballs

makes 4 servings

If you make the meatballs ahead of time, you can prepare this soup in about 20 minutes.

10 ounces trimmed lean pork loin, cut into 1" chunks

½ cup minced cilantro

¼ cup minced water chestnuts

1 tablespoon hoisin sauce

2 teaspoons reduced-sodium soy sauce

1 egg white

2 teaspoons vegetable oil

1 tablespoon minced peeled gingerroot

3 garlic cloves, minced

1 green bell pepper, seeded and diced

1 tomato, chopped

6 cups low-sodium chicken broth

2 cups Chinese broccoli* (stalks and flowers), cut into 1" pieces

1½ tablespoons cornstarch, dissolved in 2 tablespoons water

1. In a food processor, finely grind the pork. Transfer to a medium bowl; stir in the cilantro, water chestnuts, hoisin sauce, soy sauce and egg white. Shape the mixture into 36 meatballs, about ¾" each.

2. In a large nonstick saucepan, heat the oil until it just begins to smoke, 30–40 seconds. Add the ginger and garlic; cook, stirring constantly, until just fragrant (do not burn), about 15 seconds. Stir in the pepper and cook about 2 minutes; add the tomato and cook 1 minute longer.

3. Stir in the broth and bring to a boil. Reduce the heat and simmer, covered, about 10 minutes. Add the meatballs and broccoli; simmer, covered, until the meatballs are tender and cooked through, about 5 minutes. Return to a boil and stir in the dissolved cornstarch; cook, stirring constantly, until slightly thickened, about 2 minutes.

one pot

Serving provides:
1 Fruit/Vegetable,
2 Protein/Milks,
1 Fat.

Per serving:
226 Calories,
10 g Total Fat,
3 g Saturated Fat,
42 mg Cholesterol,
420 mg Sodium,
16 g Total
Carbohydrate,
2 g Dietary Fiber,
23 g Protein,
70 mg Calcium.

Points per serving: 5.

*See Glossary, page 133.

Garlic Soup

Make sure to use a bulb of garlic whose parchment-like skin is completely intact for this easy soup.

2 cups low-sodium chicken broth

1 tablespoon reduced-sodium soy sauce

¼ teaspoon salt

⅓ cup long-grain rice

1 garlic bulb, unpeeled

4 teaspoons minced peeled gingerroot

5 ounces skinless boneless chicken breast, cut into ¼" slices

2 carrots, julienned

1. In a medium nonstick saucepan, bring the broth, soy sauce, salt and 4 cups water to a boil; reduce the heat and stir in the rice, garlic and ginger. Simmer, covered, until the rice is very soft and the garlic is tender, about 45 minutes.

2. Remove the garlic from the saucepan. Cut off the stem end and squeeze the pulp into a food processor; add ¼ cup of the broth and puree. Return the garlic mixture to the saucepan and bring to a boil. Add the chicken and carrots; cook until the chicken is cooked through and the carrots are tender, about 5 minutes.

one pot

Serving provides:
1 Bread, 1 Fruit/ Vegetable, 1 Protein/ Milk.

Per serving:
140 Calories,
2 g Total Fat,
1 g Saturated Fat,
21 mg Cholesterol,
385 mg Sodium,
20 g Total Carbohydrate,
2 g Dietary Fiber,
12 g Protein,
45 mg Calcium.

Points per serving: 3.

Planning a Chinese Meal: The *Fan T'sai* Principle

Forget what's served in Chinese restaurants—most Chinese families eat quite differently. At the heart of their eating pattern is the principle of *fan t'sai*. *Fan* means "grain," and *t'sai* is "a flavorful dish." In a typical Chinese meal, *fan* is the most important element.

Whether it's rice, noodles, bread or pancakes, *fan* forms the bulk of the meal, and the flavored protein component—what Americans would consider the main course—serves only to accent the *fan*. Watch a Chinese family eat their bowls of rice, reaching out occasionally with their chopsticks to pick up some stir-fried pork and vegetables from a platter in the center of the table, and you are seeing *fan t'sai* in action.

Besides *fan*, a typical meal includes three other dishes—a meat, poultry or fish dish, a vegetable and a soup. All are served at the same time, family style, though soup is often served at the end of the meal in the emptied rice bowls.

To plan a Chinese-style meal, try to contrast flavors, textures and temperatures: For example, start with a light soup, followed by a hot spicy main dish and rice with some cold crisp vegetables. Here are some menu ideas to get you started:

Hot-and-Sour Soup with Mushrooms*
Red-Cooked Chicken with Cabbage*
Jasmine Rice
Pineapple Wedges

Spicy Cellophane Noodles*
Grilled Jade Scallops*
Dry-Cooked Green Beans*
Fortune Cookies

Steamed Vegetable Dumplings*
Noodles Topped with Five-Spice Tofu Stir-Fry*
Chilled Steamed Broccoli
Orange Wedges

Brown Rice
Spicy Tangerine Beef*
Stir-Fried Spinach*
Sliced Tart Apples

Tofu-Noodle Soup*
Rice Pancakes with Shrimp*
Steamed Asparagus
Lichees

Recipes included.

Mushroom Soup with Shredded Chicken

makes 4 servings

The rich, smoky flavor and meaty texture of shiitake mushrooms give this soup a full-bodied flavor.

¼ cup sticky rice*

10 dried Chinese black mushroom caps* (about 1 ounce)

2 tablespoons reduced-sodium soy sauce

1 tablespoon rice wine or dry sherry

2 teaspoons cornstarch

4 teaspoons Asian sesame oil

10 ounces skinless boneless chicken breasts, cut crosswise into ¼" slices

1 tablespoon minced peeled gingerroot

3 garlic cloves, minced

3 cups sliced fresh shiitake or cremini mushrooms

4 cups low-sodium chicken broth

12 asparagus spears, cut into 1" lengths

1. In a medium nonstick saucepan, combine the rice with 2 cups water; bring to a boil. Reduce the heat and simmer, covered, until tender, about 20 minutes. Drain the rice.

2. Meanwhile, in a small saucepan, bring 2 cups water to a boil. Add the black mushrooms; cover and remove from heat. Let stand until softened, about 20 minutes. Drain, reserving the liquid, and thinly slice the mushrooms. Strain the soaking liquid through a cheesecloth-lined strainer.

3. In a medium bowl, combine the soy sauce, wine, cornstarch and 2 teaspoons of the oil. Add the chicken and toss to coat.

4. In a medium nonstick saucepan, heat the remaining 2 teaspoons of the oil. Add the ginger and garlic; cook, stirring constantly, until fragrant (do not burn), about 15 seconds. Add the shiitake and black mushrooms; cook, stirring as needed, until softened, about 5 minutes. Stir in the broth and soaking liquid; bring to a boil. Reduce the heat and simmer, uncovered, about 10 minutes.

5. Stir in the chicken mixture and asparagus; simmer until the chicken is cooked through, about 5 minutes.

Serving provides:
1 Bread, 1 Fruit/Vegetable, 2 Protein/Milks, 1 Fat.

Per serving:
244 Calories, 8 g Total Fat, 2 g Saturated Fat, 41 mg Cholesterol, 468 mg Sodium, 22 g Total Carbohydrate, 3 g Dietary Fiber, 24 g Protein, 49 mg Calcium.

Points per serving: 5.

*See Glossary, page 133.

Sweet and Tangy Fish Soup

Any firm-flesh, sweet white fish—sole, flounder or halibut—makes a fine substitute for the cod.

2 teaspoons Asian sesame oil

16 scallions, sliced

2 garlic cloves, minced

½ red bell pepper, seeded and diced

2 cups bottled clam juice

3 tablespoons ketchup

1 tablespoon rice vinegar

½ teaspoon salt

½ teaspoon hot red pepper sauce

10 ounces cod fillet, cut into 1" chunks

½ cup minced cilantro

1. In a medium nonstick saucepan, heat the oil until it just begins to smoke, 30–40 seconds. Add the scallions and garlic; cook, stirring as needed, until the scallions are softened, 2–3 minutes. Add the bell pepper and cook, stirring as needed, until softened, about 5 minutes.

2. Stir in the clam juice, ketchup, vinegar, salt, pepper sauce and 2 cups water; bring to a boil. Reduce the heat and simmer, covered, until the flavors are blended, about 10 minutes. Stir in the cod and cilantro; simmer, covered, until the cod is just cooked through, about 5 minutes.

one pot

Serving provides:
1 Protein/Milk, 1 Fat.

Per serving:
108 Calories,
3 g Total Fat,
0 g Saturated Fat,
30 mg Cholesterol,
725 mg Sodium,
7 g Total Carbohydrate, 1 g Dietary Fiber, 14 g Protein,
57 mg Calcium.

Points per serving: 2.

Clam and Black Bean Soup

makes 4 servings

If the clams at your market don't look terrific, use two 10-ounce cans drained whole baby clams instead.

1 tablespoon fermented black beans*

2 teaspoons peanut or corn oil

1 ounce Chinese sausage,* thinly sliced

8 scallions, thinly sliced

1 tablespoon minced peeled gingerroot

4 garlic cloves, minced

2 tablespoons oyster sauce*

1 tablespoon reduced-sodium soy sauce

2 teaspoons sugar

1½ cups sliced Chinese broccoli*

½ red bell pepper, seeded and cut into thin strips

48 medium clams, shucked and chopped

1. In a small bowl, combine the black beans with ½ cup water; let stand until softened, about 10 minutes.

2. In a medium nonstick saucepan, heat the oil until it just begins to smoke, 30–40 seconds. Add the sausage, scallions, ginger and garlic; cook until the scallions are softened, 2–3 minutes. Add the oyster sauce, soy sauce, sugar and 3 cups water; bring to a boil. Reduce the heat and simmer, partially covered, until the flavors are blended, about 5 minutes.

3. Add the broccoli and pepper; cook until softened, about 4 minutes. Stir in the clams and beans; simmer, covered, until just cooked through, about 2 minutes.

one pot

rush hour

Serving provides:
1 Fruit/Vegetable,
2 Protein/Milks,
1 Fat.

Per serving:
181 Calories,
6 g Total Fat,
2 g Saturated Fat,
44 mg Cholesterol,
823 mg Sodium,
12 g Total
Carbohydrate,
2 g Dietary Fiber,
19 g Protein,
91 mg Calcium.

Points per serving: 4.

*See Glossary, page 133.

Tofu-Noodle Soup

If you prefer a vegetarian soup, substitute vegetable broth for the chicken broth.

¼ pound vermicelli

6 cups low-sodium chicken broth

3 tablespoons rice vinegar

2 tablespoons minced peeled gingerroot

2 tablespoons reduced-sodium soy sauce

2 carrots, thinly sliced

2 cups shredded napa, Savoy or green cabbage

¾ pound soft reduced-fat tofu, cut into 1" chunks

1 cup watercress leaves

2 teaspoons chili oil*

1. Cook the vermicelli according to package directions; drain.

2. Meanwhile, in a large saucepan, bring the broth, vinegar, ginger and soy sauce to a boil. Reduce the heat and simmer, covered, until the flavors are blended, about 5 minutes.

3. Stir in the carrots and cabbage; cook, covered, until softened, about 5 minutes. Stir in the tofu, vermicelli, watercress and oil; cook until heated through, about 3 minutes.

rush hour

Serving provides:
1 Bread, 1 Fruit/Vegetable, 1 Protein/Milk, 1 Fat.

Per serving:
219 Calories,
9 g Total Fat,
2 g Saturated Fat,
0 mg Cholesterol,
504 mg Sodium,
29 g Total Carbohydrate,
3 g Dietary Fiber,
13 g Protein,
106 mg Calcium.

Points per serving: 5.

See Glossary, page 133.

The Asian Pyramid

Like the U.S. Department of Agriculture's (USDA) Food Guide Pyramid, the Healthy Asian Pyramid is designed to help people visualize what a healthy eating pattern looks like—based on the traditional diets of China and other Asian countries. Try getting most of your foods from the bottom of the pyramid and those at the top only rarely, and you'll have a low-fat eating plan that's easy to follow.

Created by Oldways Preservation and Exchange Trust, a food and health think-tank, the Asian pyramid differs from the USDA one in several ways. First, it's very low in animal protein, with red meat eaten only monthly, and eggs and poultry just once a week. Fish or dairy products are optional daily food—indeed, in many parts of Asia, dairy products are almost never eaten.

Secondly, two-thirds of the diet comes from plant foods, with grains like rice, noodles and breads comprising the main part of each meal, followed by vegetables, fruits and legumes (beans), nuts and seeds. Fats are supplied chiefly by vegetable oils, but only in small amounts.

If that sounds like a strange way of eating, just think of a classic stir-fried dish: a heaping bed of rice with lots of vegetables and a tiny bit of shredded chicken for flavoring, or a noodle soup garnished with strips of tofu and vegetables, or dumplings filled with shredded greens and chopped peanuts. After you've tried a few Chinese meals, you'll see that eating in the Asian-pyramid pattern can be satisfying and delicious.

Egg Drop Soup

When you drizzle lightly beaten eggs into hot broth, thin wisps of egg—"egg drops"—form.

5 dried Chinese black mushrooms caps* (about ½ ounce)

5 cups low-sodium chicken broth

16 scallions, minced

2 tablespoons minced peeled gingerroot

2 tablespoons rice vinegar

2 tablespoons reduced-sodium soy sauce

4 garlic cloves, minced

3 egg whites

1 egg

1 tablespoon cornstarch, dissolved in 2 tablespoons water

Serving provides:
1 Protein/Milk,
40 Bonus Calories.

Per serving:
100 Calories,
4 g Total Fat,
1 g Saturated Fat,
53 mg Cholesterol,
507 mg Sodium,
11 g Total
Carbohydrate,
1 g Dietary Fiber,
10 g Protein,
56 mg Calcium.

Points per serving: 2.

1. In a small saucepan, bring 1 cup water to a boil. Add the mushrooms; cover and remove from heat. Let stand until softened, about 20 minutes. Drain the mushrooms, reserving the liquid. Strain the soaking liquid through a cheesecloth-lined strainer.

2. In a medium saucepan, bring the broth, scallions, the mushrooms and the soaking liquid, the ginger, vinegar, soy sauce and garlic to a boil. Reduce the heat and simmer, covered, until the flavors are blended, about 20 minutes.

3. In a small bowl, whisk the egg whites, egg and 1 tablespoon water until smooth.

4. Increase the heat and return the soup to a boil. Stir in the dissolved cornstarch and cook, stirring constantly, until slightly thickened, about 1 minute. Stir in the egg mixture and cook, stirring constantly, about 1 minute longer.

See Glossary, page 133.

Soy-Watercress Soup

makes 4 servings

This simple soup has an earthy flavor. If you prefer a vegetarian dish, make it with low-sodium vegetable broth.

2 cups low-sodium chicken broth

2 tablespoons reduced-sodium soy sauce

½ garlic clove, finely minced

¼ teaspoon grated peeled gingerroot

1 teaspoon peanut oil

1½ cups sliced shiitake mushrooms

8 scallions, thinly sliced

½ bunch watercress, tough stems removed (about 2 cups)

4 radishes, sliced paper-thin

1. In a medium saucepan, bring the broth, soy sauce, garlic, ginger and 4 cups water to a boil. Reduce the heat and simmer until the flavors are blended, about 20 minutes.

2. Meanwhile, in a medium nonstick skillet, heat the oil. Add the mushrooms and scallions; cook, stirring as needed, until the mushrooms are softened, about 10 minutes.

3. Divide the mushroom mixture among 4 bowls; top with the watercress and broth mixture. Serve, garnished with radish slices.

rush hour

Serving provides:
1 Fruit/Vegetable.

Per serving:
41 Calories,
3 g Total Fat,
1 g Saturated Fat,
0 mg Cholesterol,
369 mg Sodium,
4 g Total Carbohydrate, 1 g Dietary
Fiber, 3 g Protein,
43 mg Calcium.

Points per serving: 1.

chapter 2

NOODLES AND RICE

Pan-Fried Noodles with Spicy Lamb

makes 4 servings

Although more commonly used in Mongolian dishes, lamb takes beautifully to the Szechuan-inspired seasonings in this satisfying main dish. In order to cut the lamb as thinly as possible, partially freeze it before slicing.

2 tablespoons low-sodium chicken broth

1 tablespoon rice wine or dry sherry

1 tablespoon reduced-sodium soy sauce

2 teaspoons rice vinegar

1½ teaspoons Asian sesame oil

½ teaspoon sugar

Pinch crushed red pepper flakes

½ pound trimmed boneless lamb shoulder or leg, julienned

¼ pound thin egg noodle clusters or fideos*

1 tablespoon cornstarch

2½ teaspoons peanut oil

8 scallions, thinly sliced

1 garlic clove, minced

One ½" piece peeled gingerroot, minced

1 green bell pepper, seeded and cut into strips

½ red bell pepper, seeded and cut into strips

make ahead

spicy

Serving provides:
2 Breads, 1 Fruit/Vegetable, 1 Protein/Milk.

Per serving:
276 Calories,
10 g Total Fat,
2 g Saturated Fat,
68 mg Cholesterol,
204 mg Sodium,
29 g Total Carbohydrate,
2 g Dietary Fiber,
16 g Protein,
35 mg Calcium.

Points per serving: 6.

1. To prepare the marinade, in a gallon-size sealable plastic bag, combine the broth, wine, soy sauce, vinegar, 1 teaspoon of the sesame oil, the sugar and pepper flakes; add the lamb. Seal the bag, squeezing out the air; turn to coat the lamb. Refrigerate 1 hour, turning the bag occasionally. Drain the lamb, reserving the marinade.

2. Meanwhile, cook the noodles according to package directions. Drain and transfer to a plate. Add the remaining ½ teaspoon of the sesame oil and toss lightly; let cool.

3. In a small bowl, whisk the reserved marinade, the cornstarch and 2 tablespoons water until smooth.

4. In a large nonstick skillet or wok, heat ½ teaspoon of the peanut oil. Transfer the noodles to the skillet and cook, without stirring, about 2 minutes. Turn with a spatula and stir gently with chopsticks; cook, without stirring, about 2 minutes longer. Transfer to a serving platter, cover and keep warm.

5. Return the skillet to the heat, and heat 1 teaspoon of the peanut oil. Add the lamb and stir-fry until barely pink, 2–3 minutes; transfer to a plate and keep warm.

See Glossary, page 133.

6. Return the skillet to the heat, and heat the remaining 1 teaspoon of the peanut oil. Add the scallions, garlic and ginger; stir-fry until the scallions are softened, 2–3 minutes. Stir in both bell peppers; stir-fry until softened, about 5 minutes.

Add the lamb and the marinade mixture; bring to a rolling boil and cook until the sauce thickens and coats the lamb, about 1 minute. Pour the mixture over the cooked noodles; serve at once.

Noodle Cake with Lamb and Mushrooms

makes 4 servings

A crispy, chewy noodle cake makes a terrific base for a stir-fried dish, and it's a snap to prepare. Here, it's paired with a savory lamb topping.

2 tablespoons reduced-sodium soy sauce

1 tablespoon rice wine or dry sherry

2 teaspoons firmly packed dark brown sugar

2 garlic cloves, minced

2 star anise* cloves, or ¼ teaspoon ground anise

10 ounces trimmed boneless lean lamb shoulder or leg, cut into 1" cubes

¼ pound thin egg noodles or spaghettini

1 teaspoon Asian sesame oil

3 teaspoons peanut oil

4 scallions, thinly sliced

One ½" piece peeled gingerroot, minced

2 cups thinly sliced mushrooms

1 carrot, julienned

1 cup thinly sliced napa cabbage

2 teaspoons cornstarch, dissolved in ¼ cup water

*See Glossary, page 133.

make ahead

Serving provides:
2 Breads, 1 Fruit/
Vegetable, 2 Protein/
Milks, 1 Fat.

Per serving:
313 Calories,
11 g Total Fat,
3 g Saturated Fat,
77 mg Cholesterol,
371 mg Sodium,
33 g Total
Carbohydrate,
2 g Dietary Fiber,
20 g Protein,
55 mg Calcium.

Points per serving: 7.

1. To prepare the marinade, in a gallon-size sealable plastic bag, combine the soy sauce, wine, brown sugar, garlic and anise; add the lamb. Seal the bag, squeezing out the air; turn to coat the lamb. Refrigerate at least 2 hours, turning the bag occasionally. Drain the lamb, reserving the marinade.

2. Meanwhile, cook the noodles according to package directions. Drain and transfer to an 8" round cake pan. Add the sesame oil; toss lightly and spread evenly to form a smooth top. Let cool to form a round cake.

3. In a large nonstick skillet, heat 1 teaspoon of the peanut oil. Invert the noodle cake into the skillet and cook until golden brown, about 2 minutes on each side. Transfer to a serving platter and keep warm.

4. Return the skillet to the heat, and heat 1 more teaspoon of the peanut oil. Add the lamb; cook, stirring as needed, until barely pink, 2–3 minutes. Transfer to a plate and keep warm. Wipe out the skillet with a paper towel.

5. Return the skillet to the heat, and heat the remaining 1 teaspoon of the peanut oil. Add the scallions and ginger; cook, stirring as needed, until the scallions are softened, 2–3 minutes. Add the

mushrooms and carrot; cook, stirring as needed, until the mushrooms have released and then reabsorbed their liquid and the carrot is softened, 6–8 minutes.

6. Stir in the cabbage and ¼ cup water; bring to a boil and cook until the cabbage is softened, about 2 minutes. Stir in the dissolved cornstarch; cook until the sauce is thickened, about 1 minute. Stir in the lamb and heat through 1 minute. Pour the lamb mixture over the noodle cake; serve at once.

A Regional Taste Tour

We tend to think of Chinese food as one cuisine, but dishes and cooking styles vary as widely as do the terrains in this vast country. Here's what you can expect from each region—and your best bets for light eating.

Northern (Beijing or Mandarin, Mongolian):

Here, wheat is the staple crop, so most dishes center on noodles and pancakes. Meats are often prominent—particularly beef and lamb, but not pork, since this region has a large Muslim population. Look for boiled and roasted dishes, but do watch out for heavy sauces.

Southern (Cantonese):

With a year-round growing season and proximity to the sea, this region is blessed with outstanding vegetables, fruits and fish. Chefs rarely use heavy sauces since the ingredients are so fresh, and healthy cooking techniques like steaming, roasting and simmering are common. For instant portion control, try *dim sum*—little dishes of dumplings, noodles and other savories—but resist the temptation to order seconds.

Eastern (Shanghai):

Subtropical climates make "the land of fish and rice" abundant also in vegetables, and its vegetarian dishes can be spectacular. Seasonings tend to be delicate and light, but watch out for red-cooked dishes (simmered with soy sauce and sugar).

Western (Szechuan, Hunan):

Most dishes in this "land of abundance" revolve around rice and feature spicy-hot and intense flavorings. While steaming and stir-frying are popular, fried items or nuts can turn a healthful dish into a fat trap.

Cellophane Noodles with Spicy Ground Pork

makes 4 servings

In China, this classic side dish (or lunch entrée) is imaginatively named "Ants on a Tree" since the bits of ground pork against the light noodles look something like ants climbing on tree bark. For truly lean ground pork, start with a well-trimmed lean cut like loin and grind it in your food processor.

one pot

spicy

Serving provides:
1 Bread, 1 Protein/ Milk, 1 Fat.

Per serving:
173 Calories,
6 g Total Fat,
2 g Saturated Fat,
23 mg Cholesterol,
337 mg Sodium,
22 g Total Carbohydrate,
1 g Dietary Fiber,
8 g Protein,
23 mg Calcium.

Points per serving: 4.

5 ounces lean ground pork

1 tablespoon reduced-sodium soy sauce

1 tablespoon ketchup

2 teaspoons hoisin sauce

1 teaspoon rice vinegar

2 garlic cloves, minced

¼ pound cellophane noodles*

2 teaspoons peanut oil

2 scallions, minced

½ teaspoon minced peeled gingerroot

1 teaspoon hot chili paste*

1 cup low-sodium chicken broth

1 tablespoon minced cilantro

1. In a medium bowl, combine the pork, soy sauce, ketchup, hoisin sauce, vinegar and garlic; stir lightly to blend well. Refrigerate, covered, until the flavors are blended, about 20 minutes.

2. Meanwhile, place the cellophane noodles in a medium bowl with enough hot water to cover. Let stand until softened, about 10 minutes; drain.

3. In a large nonstick skillet or wok, heat 1 teaspoon of the oil. Add the pork mixture and cook, stirring to break up the meat, until cooked through, about 4 minutes. Transfer the pork and pan juices to a plate and keep warm. Wipe out the skillet with a paper towel.

4. Return the skillet to the heat, and heat the remaining 1 teaspoon of the oil 30 seconds. Add the scallions and ginger; cook, stirring as needed, until just fragrant (do not burn), about 15 seconds. Add the chili paste and cook 5 seconds longer. Add the pork, noodles and broth; bring to a boil. Reduce the heat and simmer, stirring gently, until the noodles have absorbed most of the liquid, 3–4 minutes. Sprinkle with the cilantro; serve at once.

*See Glossary, page 133.

Stir-Fried Rice Noodles with Chicken, Mushrooms and Leeks

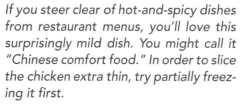

makes 4 servings

If you steer clear of hot-and-spicy dishes from restaurant menus, you'll love this surprisingly mild dish. You might call it "Chinese comfort food." In order to slice the chicken extra thin, try partially freezing it first.

1 tablespoon rice wine or dry sherry

2 teaspoons reduced-sodium soy sauce

1 teaspoon cornstarch

1 teaspoon Asian sesame oil

5 ounces skinless boneless chicken breast, cut into 2 x ¼" strips

¼ pound thin rice noodles

3 teaspoons peanut oil

2 garlic cloves, minced

½ teaspoon minced peeled gingerroot

2 leeks, cleaned and thinly sliced

1 cup thinly sliced shiitake mushrooms

½ red bell pepper, seeded and diced

½ cup low-sodium chicken broth

1. To prepare the marinade, in a quart-size sealable plastic bag, combine the wine, soy sauce, cornstarch and sesame oil; add the chicken. Seal the bag, squeezing out the air; turn to coat the chicken. Refrigerate at least 30 minutes, turning the bag occasionally. Drain the chicken, reserving the marinade.

2. Meanwhile, place the rice noodles in a large bowl with enough hot water to cover. Let stand until softened, about 20 minutes; drain.

3. In a large nonstick skillet or wok, heat 2 teaspoons of the peanut oil. Add the chicken in batches and cook, stirring constantly, until no longer pink, 2–3 minutes. Transfer the chicken and pan juices to a plate and keep warm. Wipe out the skillet with a paper towel.

4. Return the skillet to the heat, and heat the remaining 1 teaspoon of the peanut oil. Add the garlic and ginger; cook, stirring constantly, until just fragrant (do not burn), about 15 seconds. Add the leeks, mushrooms and pepper; cook, stirring as needed, until the leeks are softened, 7–8 minutes. Add the broth and the marinade; bring to a boil. Stir in the chicken and noodles; cook, tossing gently, until the noodles have absorbed the sauce, 2–3 minutes; serve at once.

one pot

Serving provides:
1 Bread, 1 Fruit/
Vegetable, 1 Protein/
Milk, 1 Fat.

Per serving:
232 Calories,
5 g Total Fat,
1 g Saturated Fat,
21 mg Cholesterol,
152 mg Sodium,
33 g Total
Carbohydrate,
1 g Dietary Fiber,
11 g Protein,
43 mg Calcium.

Points per serving: 5.

(See photo insert.)

Curried Noodles with Shrimp

makes 4 servings

This colorful version of the Singapore Noodles found on many Chinese restaurant menus is full of textures and flavors. Serve it piping hot or, as the Chinese often do, at room temperature.

¼ pound spaghettini

1 teaspoon Asian sesame oil

1 cup low-sodium chicken broth

2 teaspoons cornstarch

½ teaspoon cinnamon

¼ teaspoon coconut extract

3 teaspoons peanut oil

1 tablespoon curry powder

½ pound medium shrimp, peeled and deveined

½ onion, diced

1 carrot, diced and steamed

1 cup thawed frozen peas

1 cup chopped cleaned spinach (bite-size pieces)

1. Cook the noodles according to package directions. Drain in a colander, rinsing with warm water; place in a serving bowl. Add the sesame oil and toss lightly; keep warm.

2. In a small bowl, whisk the broth, cornstarch, cinnamon and coconut extract until smooth.

3. In a large nonstick skillet or wok, heat 2 teaspoons of the peanut oil. Add the curry and cook, stirring constantly, until just fragrant (do not burn), about 30 seconds. Add the shrimp and stir-fry until just opaque, 2–3 minutes. Transfer to a plate and keep warm.

4. Return the skillet to the heat, and heat the remaining 1 teaspoon of the peanut oil. Add the onion and stir-fry until softened, about 5 minutes. Stir in the broth mixture, the carrot, peas and spinach; cook until the spinach is wilted and the sauce is slightly thickened, about 1 minute. Stir in the noodles and shrimp; toss to coat.

rush hour

Serving provides:
2 Breads, 1 Fruit/ Vegetable, 1 Protein/ Milk, 1 Fat.

Per serving:
291 Calories,
8 g Total Fat,
1 g Saturated Fat,
116 mg Cholesterol,
198 mg Sodium,
36 g Total Carbohydrate,
4 g Dietary Fiber,
20 g Protein,
90 mg Calcium.

Points per serving: 6.

Chinese Spicy Beans and Noodles

makes 4 servings

Sometimes called yard-long beans, Chinese long green beans resemble regular green beans—except for their length. They are most often picked when they are about 18 inches long, and are usually cut to 2" lengths before cooking. Their peak season is fall, but they're usually available in Asian markets year-round. Feel free to substitute with regular green beans.

4 cups Chinese long green beans, trimmed and cut into 2" lengths

½ teaspoon salt

6 ounces spaghettini

4 teaspoons Asian sesame oil

1 red bell pepper, seeded and julienned

3 garlic cloves, minced

½ cup low-sodium chicken broth

½ teaspoon crushed red pepper flakes

1. In a large pot of boiling water, cook the beans with the salt until just tender, 5–7 minutes. With a slotted spoon or tongs, transfer the beans to a large serving bowl; keep warm.

2. In the same pot of boiling water, cook the spaghettini according to package directions. Drain and add to the beans.

3. In a medium nonstick skillet, heat the oil. Add the bell pepper and garlic; cook, stirring as needed, until the bell pepper is softened, about 5 minutes. Add the broth and pepper flakes; simmer 3–5 minutes. Pour over the beans and noodles; toss to coat.

rush hour

spicy

Serving provides:
2 Breads, 1 Fruit/ Vegetable, 1 Fat.

Per serving:
250 Calories,
7 g Total Fat,
1 g Saturated Fat,
40 mg Cholesterol,
304 mg Sodium,
41 g Total Carbohydrate,
4 g Dietary Fiber,
9 g Protein,
64 mg Calcium.

Points per serving: 5.

Spicy Cellophane Noodles

makes 4 servings

one pot

rush hour

spicy

Serving provides:
1 Bread, 1 Fruit/
Vegetable, 1 Protein/
Milk, 1 Fat.

Per serving:
189 Calories,
6 g Total Fat,
1 g Saturated Fat,
0 mg Cholesterol,
651 mg Sodium,
29 g Total
Carbohydrate,
1 g Dietary Fiber,
5 g Protein,
51 mg Calcium.

Points per serving: 4.

Use firm tofu in dishes like this, or in stir-fried or grilled dishes—where it's important that it keep its shape. Soft tofu is ideal for recipes in which it's blended or mashed.

¼ pound cellophane noodles*

½ pound firm reduced-fat tofu, diced

4 teaspoons Asian sesame oil

2 garlic cloves, minced

1 red bell pepper, seeded and cut into thin strips

1 green bell pepper, seeded and cut into thin strips

1 scallion, sliced

¼ cup reduced-sodium soy sauce

1 tablespoon rice vinegar

1 tablespoon honey

½ jalapeño or serrano chile pepper, seeded, deveined and minced (wear gloves to prevent irritation)

½ teaspoon five-spice powder*

2 teaspoons sesame seeds, toasted†

1. Place the cellophane noodles in a large bowl with enough hot water to cover. Let stand until softened, about 10 minutes; drain and return to the bowl. Stir in the tofu.

2. Meanwhile, in a large nonstick skillet, heat the oil. Add the garlic and cook, stirring constantly, until golden, about 2 minutes. Add the bell peppers and scallion; cook, stirring as needed, until softened, about 5 minutes. Add to the tofu mixture; toss to combine.

3. To prepare the dressing, in a small jar with a tight-fitting lid or in a small bowl, combine the soy sauce, vinegar, honey, jalapeño and five-spice powder; cover and shake well or, with a wire whisk, blend until combined. Pour over the noodles; toss to coat. Sprinkle with the sesame seeds.

---

*See Glossary, page 133.

†To toast the sesame seeds, in a small nonstick skillet, cook the sesame seeds, stirring constantly, until lightly browned, 1–2 minutes. Immediately transfer to a heat-resistant plate to cool.

Cold Noodles with Tofu-Peanut Sauce

makes 4 servings

Our take on the restaurant favorite Cold Noodles with Sesame Sauce is easy to make at home. Replacing some of the peanut butter with tofu adds a little protein and cuts the fat considerably.

one pot

rush hour

Serving provides:
2 Breads, 1 Protein/
Milk, 1 Fat.

Per serving:
232 Calories,
9 g Total Fat,
1 g Saturated Fat,
30 mg Cholesterol,
212 mg Sodium,
28 g Total
Carbohydrate,
2 g Dietary Fiber,
9 g Protein,
32 mg Calcium.

Points per serving: 5.

¼ pound spaghettini

1 teaspoon Asian sesame oil

3 tablespoons low-sodium chicken broth

3 tablespoons natural peanut butter

1 ounce firm reduced-fat tofu

1 tablespoon rice vinegar

1 tablespoon reduced-sodium soy sauce

1 teaspoon sugar

½ teaspoon minced peeled gingerroot

½ cup bean sprouts

½ cucumber, peeled, seeded and
    julienned

2 scallions, halved lengthwise and cut
    into 1" lengths

1 tablespoon minced fresh cilantro

Pinch crushed red pepper flakes
    (optional)

1. Cook the spaghettini according to package directions. Drain in a colander, rinsing with cold water; place in a serving bowl. Add the sesame oil and toss lightly.

2. Meanwhile, to prepare the dressing, in a blender or food processor, puree the broth, peanut butter, tofu, vinegar, soy sauce, sugar and ginger.

3. Scatter the bean sprouts, cucumber and scallions over the noodles; pour the dressing over and toss lightly to coat. Sprinkle with the cilantro and pepper flakes (if using).

Vegetable Lo Mein

makes 4 servings

The many colors and textures in this hearty main dish make it especially pleasing to the eye and palate.

5 dried Chinese black mushroom caps* (about ½ ounce)

¼ pound thin egg noodle clusters or fideos*

1 teaspoon Asian sesame oil

1 tablespoon hoisin sauce

1 tablespoon reduced-sodium soy sauce

1 tablespoon rice vinegar

Pinch crushed red pepper flakes

1 teaspoon peanut oil

One ½" piece peeled gingerroot, minced

1 garlic clove, minced

8 scallions, thinly sliced

½ red bell pepper, seeded and cut into thin strips

1 celery stalk, sliced into thin crescents

2 cups thinly sliced bok choy (Chinese cabbage)

½ cup drained rinsed canned sliced bamboo shoots

¼ cup unsalted dry-roasted peanuts, chopped

2 tablespoons minced cilantro

vegetarian

Serving provides:
2 Breads, 1 Fruit/Vegetable, 1 Fat.

Per serving:
225 Calories,
7 g Total Fat,
1 g Saturated Fat,
30 mg Cholesterol,
270 mg Sodium,
33 g Total Carbohydrate,
4 g Dietary Fiber,
8 g Protein,
71 mg Calcium.

Points per serving: 4.

1. In a small saucepan, bring 1 cup water to a boil; add the mushrooms. Cover and remove from heat. Let stand until softened, about 20 minutes. Drain, discarding the liquid, and thinly slice the mushrooms.

2. Meanwhile, cook the noodles according to package directions. Drain in a colander, rinsing with warm water; place in a serving bowl. Add the sesame oil and toss lightly.

3. In a small bowl, combine the hoisin sauce, soy sauce, vinegar, pepper flakes and 3 tablespoons water.

4. In a large nonstick skillet, heat the peanut oil. Add the ginger and garlic; cook, stirring constantly, until just fragrant (do not burn), about 15 seconds. Stir in the scallions, bell pepper and celery; stir-fry until the vegetables are softened, 5–8 minutes. Add the bok choy, bamboo shoots and the mushrooms; continue cooking, stirring gently, until the bok choy is wilted, 3–4 minutes. Stir in the noodles and the hoisin sauce mixture; cook, stirring gently, until the noodles have absorbed the sauce, 2–3 minutes. Sprinkle with the peanuts and cilantro.

See Glossary, page 133.

Steamed Rice

makes 6 servings

Steaming produces a lighter, fluffier rice than does the conventional boiling method. Similar results can be achieved with an electric rice cooker, a staple in many Chinese homes.

1 cup long-grain raw (not converted) white rice

1. Place the rice in a strainer. Under cold running water, rinse well, stirring with your fingers, until the water runs clear.

2. In a medium, heavy saucepan, combine the rice with enough cold water to cover; bring to a boil. Reduce the heat and simmer, about 5 minutes; drain.

3. Line a steamer rack with moistened cheesecloth; add the partially cooked rice and spread into an even layer.

4. In a large saucepan or wok, bring 3" of water to a boil. Place the steamer rack in the saucepan and cover with a tight-fitting lid; reduce the heat and steam the rice, about 30 minutes. Remove from heat and let stand about 10 minutes. Fluff with a fork or chopsticks; serve at once.

make ahead

vegetarian

Serving provides:
1 Bread.

Per serving:
103 Calories,
0 g Total Fat,
0 g Saturated Fat,
0 mg Cholesterol,
1 mg Sodium,
23 g Total
Carbohydrate,
0 g Dietary Fiber,
2 g Protein,
8 mg Calcium.

Points per serving: 2.

Beyond Basic White: A Rice Primer

America's favorite, long-grain white rice, is versatile and tasty—but it gets boring very fast. In China, most cooks have in their kitchens a variety of rices to suit different types of dishes. Why not expand *your* rice repertoire with tasty options like these?

Brown Rice:

Chewy and nutty tasting, brown rice has its bran layers still intact—and twice the fiber content of white rice. It's also richer in vitamin E and magnesium. Since it takes nearly twice as long to cook as does basic white, make an extra batch to keep in the refrigerator or freezer for quick meals later. It can be easily substituted for white rice in recipes.

Short-Grain or Sticky Rice:

When cooked, this rice is softer and stickier than is long-grain, making it ideal for forming into patties or for rolling in wrappers and steaming. In Taiwan, sticky rice is the choice for daily menus.

Sweet or Glutinous Rice:

This very-short-grain rice is rich in a starch called amylopectin, which makes it extremely sticky and soft when cooked. It's most commonly used in desserts such as puddings. If unavailable, substitute Arborio or Valencia rice.

Jasmine and Basmati Rice:

Both of these aromatic long-grain rices have a wonderful popcorn-like scent and flavor. Use them interchangeably with white rice; they'll add an extra depth of flavor.

Five-Treasure Rice

makes 4 servings

The "treasures" in this tasty fried rice dish can vary with what you have on hand. If you have leftover cooked meats or fish, substitute them for the chicken and shrimp; use peanuts instead of walnuts— or try drained rinsed canned black beans instead of the peas. It's delicious almost any way!

2 tablespoons low-sodium chicken broth

1 tablespoon reduced-sodium soy sauce

1 tablespoon rice wine or dry sherry

1 teaspoon cornstarch

Pinch ground white pepper

Pinch five-spice powder* (optional)

2 cups cold cooked long-grain white or brown rice

2 teaspoons peanut oil

4 scallions, sliced

One ½" piece peeled gingerroot, minced

1 cup thawed frozen peas

¼ pound small shrimp, cooked and peeled

½ cup shredded cooked skinless chicken breast

2 egg whites, beaten

¼ cup walnuts, toasted†

1. In a small bowl, whisk the broth, soy sauce, wine, cornstarch, pepper and five-spice powder (if using) until smooth.

2. Place the rice in a shallow bowl; with moistened fingers, mix to separate the grains.

3. In a large nonstick skillet or wok, heat the oil. Add the scallions and ginger; cook, stirring constantly, until the scallions are softened, 2–3 minutes. Add the peas, shrimp, chicken, egg whites and the broth mixture; cook, stirring constantly, until the egg whites are cooked, about 3 minutes. Stir in the rice and cook, tossing gently, until heated through, 2–3 minutes. Sprinkle with the walnuts; serve at once.

*See Glossary, page 133.

†To toast the walnuts, preheat the oven to 350° F. Spread the walnuts in a shallow baking pan; bake, stirring as needed, until golden brown, 8–10 minutes.

one pot

rush hour

Serving provides:
2 Breads, 1 Protein/ Milk, 1 Fat.

Per serving:
259 Calories,
8 g Total Fat,
1 g Saturated Fat,
67 mg Cholesterol,
299 mg Sodium,
28 g Total Carbohydrate,
2 g Dietary Fiber,
17 g Protein,
44 mg Calcium.

Points per serving: 5.

Curried Fried Rice

makes 4 servings

Curry powder may seem more Indian than Chinese, but Cantonese cooks have long been familiar with this aromatic flavoring. Remember to start with cold rice or it will stick to the pan!

3 cups cold cooked long-grain white or brown rice

4 teaspoons peanut oil

8 scallions, thinly sliced

2 teaspoons curry powder

2 carrots, diced and steamed

1 cup steamed chopped green beans

½ cup diced lean turkey ham

one pot

rush hour

Serving provides:
2 Breads, 1 Fruit/
Vegetable, 1 Fat.

Per serving:
239 Calories,
6 g Total Fat,
1 g Saturated Fat,
9 mg Cholesterol,
165 mg Sodium,
40 g Total
Carbohydrate,
3 g Dietary Fiber,
7 g Protein,
56 mg Calcium.

Points per serving: 5.

(See photo insert.)

1. Place the rice in a shallow bowl; with moistened fingers, mix to separate the grains.

2. In a large nonstick saucepan, heat the oil. Add the scallions and cook, stirring as needed, until softened, 2–3 minutes. Add the curry and cook, stirring constantly, until just fragrant (do not burn), about 30 seconds. Add the carrots, green beans and ham; cook, tossing lightly, about 1 minute. Stir in the rice and 2 tablespoons water; cook, tossing gently to combine, until the rice is thoroughly coated. Serve at once.

Rice Pancakes with Shrimp

makes 4 servings

These delightful pancakes look just like ordinary flapjacks—until you taste them. Inspired by the scallion pancakes often served for breakfast throughout China, they're made with cooked rice. Enjoy them plain or with a sprinkling of reduced-sodium soy sauce. The recipe doubles easily.

½ cup cooked white rice

½ cup low-fat (1%) milk

1 egg

3 tablespoons all-purpose flour

1 tablespoon reduced-sodium soy sauce

1 teaspoon Asian sesame oil

½ teaspoon baking soda

1 teaspoon peanut oil

4 scallions, sliced

¼ pound small shrimp, cooked, peeled and halved lengthwise

1 tablespoon minced cilantro

1. In a food processor or blender, puree the rice, milk, egg, flour, soy sauce and sesame oil to make a smooth, thin batter. Add the baking soda and pulse once or twice to blend.

2. In a small nonstick skillet, heat the peanut oil. Add the scallions and cook, stirring as needed until softened, 2–3 minutes. Stir the scallions into the batter, then stir in the shrimp. Wipe out the skillet with a paper towel.

3. Spray the skillet with nonstick cooking spray; heat. Pour one-fourth of the batter into the skillet, tilting to cover the bottom of the pan. Cook until the underside is set, about 1 minute. Carefully turn and cook the other side until lightly browned, 30–45 seconds. Slide the pancake onto a plate and keep warm. Repeat with the remaining batter, spraying the skillet with nonstick cooking spray between each batch, to make 4 pancakes. Sprinkle each pancake with the cilantro; serve at once.

one pot

rush hour

Serving provides:
1 Bread, 1 Protein/
Milk, 1 Fat.

Per serving:
146 Calories,
5 g Total Fat,
1 g Saturated Fat,
110 mg Cholesterol,
403 mg Sodium,
14 g Total
Carbohydrate,
0 g Dietary Fiber,
10 g Protein,
64 mg Calcium.

Points per serving: 3.

Rice Casserole with Tempeh and Mushrooms

makes 8 servings

This deliciously homey vegetarian casserole takes advantage of the meaty flavors of Chinese mushrooms and tempeh (fermented soybean cake, available in natural food stores). It's also wonderful if reheated a day later.

make ahead

vegetarian

Serving provides:
1 Bread, 1 Fruit/
Vegetable, 1 Fat.

Per serving:
192 Calories,
4 g Total Fat,
1 g Saturated Fat,
0 mg Cholesterol,
113 mg Sodium,
32 g Total
Carbohydrate,
3 g Dietary Fiber,
6 g Protein,
51 mg Calcium.

Points per serving: 4.

5 dried Chinese black mushroom caps*
   (about ½ ounce)

1⅓ cups brown rice

2 carrots, diced

1 tablespoon reduced-sodium soy sauce

¼ pound tempeh,* crumbled

2 teaspoons peanut oil

1 garlic clove, minced

One ½" piece peeled gingerroot, minced

1 red bell pepper, seeded and chopped

2 cups thinly sliced bok choy (Chinese
   cabbage)

2 tablespoons rice wine or dry sherry

1 teaspoon sugar

6 asparagus spears, cut into 3" pieces

1½ cups low-sodium vegetable broth

2 teaspoons Asian sesame oil

1. In a small saucepan, bring 1 cup water to a boil; add the mushrooms. Cover and remove from heat. Let stand until softened, about 20 minutes. Drain, discarding the liquid, and thinly slice the mushrooms.

2. Place the rice in a strainer. Under cold running water, rinse well, stirring with your fingers, until the water runs clear.

3. In a 2-quart flameproof casserole or Dutch oven, combine 2 cups water and the rice; bring to a boil. Stir in the carrots, the mushrooms and soy sauce; reduce the heat and simmer, covered, until the vegetables are tender, about 20 minutes. Stir in the tempeh.

4. Preheat the oven to 350° F.

5. In a large nonstick skillet or wok, heat the peanut oil. Add the garlic and ginger; stir-fry until just fragrant (do not burn), about 15 seconds. Add the pepper; stir-fry until softened, about 5 minutes. Transfer the pepper to a plate and return the skillet to the heat; add the bok choy and stir-fry until softened, 1–2 minutes. Stir in the wine and sugar.

6. In the casserole, arrange the asparagus, the pepper and bok choy over the rice in separate piles. Pour the broth and sesame oil over the rice; bake, covered, until the rice is tender and the liquid is absorbed, 20–25 minutes.

See Glossary, page 133.

Sizzling Rice

one pot

make ahead

vegetarian

Serving provides:
2 Breads.

Per serving:
155 Calories,
0 g Total Fat,
0 g Saturated Fat,
0 mg Cholesterol,
2 mg Sodium,
34 g Total
Carbohydrate,
0 g Dietary Fiber,
3 g Protein,
12 mg Calcium.

Points per serving: 3.

If you've ever heard the dramatic sound of a sizzling rice dish being brought to the table in a Chinese restaurant, you'll be thrilled to discover that you can recreate the excitement at home. Although the process is a bit time-consuming, this crispy rice (which becomes chewy when you add a hot sauce) can be made well in advance. Just before serving, simply fry it in a little oil until lightly browned, then top with a sauced dish and listen! For inspiration, see Pungent Vegetables over Sizzling Rice (page 35).

1½ cups long-grain white rice

1. Place the rice in a strainer. Under cold running water, rinse well, stirring with your fingers, until the water runs clear. Spread the rice evenly into a 10 x 8" baking pan; add 2 cups cold water and cover the pan with foil. Let soak about 40 minutes.

2. Preheat the oven to 350° F.

3. Bake the undrained rice, covered, about 30 minutes; uncover and press the rice with a spatula to flatten. Reduce the oven heat to 200° F; return the rice to the oven and continue baking, uncovered, until completely dry, 8–9 hours or overnight. With a fork, break the rice into clumps. Use immediately or store in an airtight container up to 2 months.

Pungent Vegetables over Sizzling Rice

makes 6 servings

A show-stopping dish that really wakes up the palate: hot, spicy vegetables poured over chewy-crisp rice make a sizzling presentation.

spicy

vegetarian

Serving provides:
2 Breads, 1 Fruit/
Vegetable, 1 Fat.

Per serving:
227 Calories,
5 g Total Fat,
1 g Saturated Fat,
0 mg Cholesterol,
156 mg Sodium,
41 g Total
Carbohydrate,
2 g Dietary Fiber,
5 g Protein,
61 mg Calcium.

Points per serving: 5.

5 dried Chinese black mushroom caps*
  (about ½ ounce)

6 teaspoons peanut oil

3 cups thinly sliced bok choy (Chinese
  cabbage)

1½ cups julienned daikon radish*

1 red bell pepper, seeded and cut into
  ¼" strips

One ½" piece peeled gingerroot,
  minced

1 garlic clove, minced

½–1 teaspoon hot chili paste*

1 cup drained rinsed canned sliced
  bamboo shoots

½ cup low-sodium vegetable broth

2 tablespoons white vinegar

1 tablespoon reduced-sodium soy sauce

1 teaspoon sugar

4½ cups Sizzling Rice (page 34)

1. In a small saucepan, bring 1 cup water to a boil; add the mushrooms. Cover and remove from heat. Let stand until softened, about 20 minutes. Drain, discarding the liquid, and thinly slice the mushrooms.

2. In a large nonstick skillet or wok, heat 2 teaspoons of the oil. Add the bok choy, radish and pepper; cook, stirring as needed, until softened, 6–8 minutes. Transfer to a plate and keep warm. Reserve the cooking liquid in the skillet.

3. Return the skillet to the heat. Add the ginger and garlic; cook, stirring as needed, until just fragrant (do not burn), about 15 seconds. Add the chili paste and cook about 5 seconds. Stir in the mushrooms, bamboo shoots, broth, vinegar, soy sauce and sugar; cook, stirring gently, until heated through, 2–3 minutes. Add the bok choy mixture and cook 1 minute.

4. Meanwhile, in another large nonstick skillet or wok, heat the remaining 4 teaspoons of the oil until it just begins to smoke, 30–40 seconds. Add the rice and cook, stirring as needed, until lightly golden, 2–3 minutes.

5. To serve, immediately pour the hot vegetable mixture over the rice in the skillet, creating a sizzling sound; serve at once.

See Glossary, page 133.

Soy Sauce Rice

makes 6 servings

This simplest of flavored rice dishes makes a tasty accompaniment to a stir-fry. For a satisfying main dish on its own, double the portion size and toss in a handful of chopped cooked vegetables and some shredded cooked chicken or crumbled tofu.

1 cup long-grain white rice

8 scallions, thinly sliced

¼ cup diced pimiento

2 tablespoons reduced-sodium soy sauce

1 tablespoon peanut oil

½ teaspoon sugar

1. Place the rice in a strainer. Under cold running water, rinse well, stirring with your fingers, until the water runs clear.

2. In a medium nonstick saucepan, combine 1¾ cups water and the rice; cover and bring to a boil. Reduce the heat and simmer about 20 minutes. Remove from the heat and let stand, covered, about 20 minutes longer.

3. Fluff the rice with a fork or chopsticks; stir in the scallions, pimiento, soy sauce, oil and sugar.

one pot

vegetarian

Serving provides:
1 Bread, 1 Fat.

Per serving:
133 Calories,
2 g Total Fat,
0 g Saturated Fat,
0 mg Cholesterol,
204 mg Sodium,
25 g Total
Carbohydrate,
1 g Dietary Fiber,
3 g Protein,
16 mg Calcium.

Points per serving: 3.

chapter 3

WRAPPED DISHES

Beef-Stuffed Cabbage Rolls

makes 4 servings

To cut down on fat and to lighten the flavor, use ground skinless chicken or turkey.

5 dried Chinese black mushroom caps* (about ½ ounce)

½ pound lean ground beef (10% or less fat)

1 egg, lightly beaten

2 tablespoons minced cilantro

2 scallions, minced

2 teaspoons Asian sesame oil

2 teaspoons orange marmalade

1 teaspoon grated orange zest

1 teaspoon garlic-chili sauce

½ teaspoon salt

24 small napa or Savoy cabbage leaves, center ribs removed

make ahead

Serving provides:
1 Fruit/Vegetable,
2 Protein/Milks,
1 Fat.

Per serving:
178 Calories,
10 g Total Fat,
3 g Saturated Fat,
93 mg Cholesterol,
363 mg Sodium,
7 g Total Carbohydrate, 1 g Dietary Fiber, 16 g Protein,
60 mg Calcium.

Points per serving: 4.

1. In a small saucepan, bring 1 cup water to a boil; add the black mushrooms. Cover and remove from heat. Let stand until softened, about 20 minutes. Drain, reserving ¼ cup liquid, and coarsely chop the mushrooms. Strain the soaking liquid through a cheesecloth-lined strainer into a medium bowl.

2. Add the beef, egg, cilantro, scallions, oil, marmalade, orange zest, chili sauce and salt to the soaking liquid. Stir in the mushrooms.

3. In a large pot of boiling water, cook the cabbage leaves until tender and pliable, about 3 minutes. Drain and place on paper towels. When cool enough to handle, spoon 1 generous tablespoon of the beef mixture into the center of each leaf; fold in the ends and roll up jelly-roll fashion.

4. In a large saucepan, bring 2" of water to a boil. Arrange the cabbage rolls, seam-side down, on a steamer rack and place in the saucepan; cover with a tight-fitting lid. Reduce the heat and steam until cooked through, about 7 minutes.

See Glossary, page 133.

China versus the U.S.: How We Compare

China is on the other side of the world from the U.S. and worlds away in its eating patterns. Though it's impossible to generalize about a country that includes 20 provinces and a huge range of climates and cultures, a major diet survey provides some information about how people eat throughout China—and about how these patterns compare to those most Americans follow. Here is a snapshot of some of the most important differences:

- On average, most Chinese diets provide about 15 percent of calories from fat and only 7 percent come from artery-damaging saturated fat. By contrast, the average American diet consists of 34 percent of calories coming from fat, and 13 of them are from saturated fat. Not surprisingly, the Chinese have one of the world's lowest heart-disease rates and Americans one of the highest.

- The total caloric intake of most Chinese people is about 20 percent higher than that of Americans—yet in general, Americans are 25 percent fatter. Lower rates of physical activity in the U.S. may explain the difference, along with our higher-fat diets.

- The Chinese tend to eat more than three times as much fiber than do Americans, perhaps one reason why the Chinese rates of colon cancer are about one-third as high as ours.

- The Chinese have higher rates of stroke than do Americans, possibly because smoking in Asia is more common. Their stomach-cancer rates are also higher; experts blame the high consumption of pickled and salted foods, which can contain cancer-causing mold toxins.

Shrimp-Stuffed Swiss Chard Rolls

makes 4 servings

Swiss chard is actually a beet—it's grown for its succulent stalk and broad leaves, rather than its roots.

20 well-washed Swiss chard leaves

4 sun-dried tomato halves (not oil-packed)

¼ pound large shrimp, peeled, deveined and finely chopped

8 scallions, minced

¼ cup minced water chestnuts

1 tablespoon rice wine or dry sherry

2 teaspoons Asian sesame oil

½ teaspoon ground ginger

½ teaspoon salt

1 tablespoon cornstarch

½ egg white

¼ cup unsalted dry-roasted peanuts, coarsely chopped

¼ cup minced cilantro

one pot

Serving provides:
2 Fruit/Vegetables,
1 Protein/Milk, 1 Fat.

Per serving:
140 Calories,
6 g Total Fat,
1 g Saturated Fat,
43 mg Cholesterol,
481 mg Sodium,
11 g Total
Carbohydrate,
3 g Dietary Fiber,
10 g Protein,
72 mg Calcium.

Points per serving: 3.

1. In a large pot of boiling water, cook the chard leaves until tender and pliable, about 3 minutes. With tongs, transfer them to paper towels to drain.

2. In the same pot of boiling water, cook the tomatoes until softened, about 4 minutes. Drain the tomatoes on paper towels, then coarsely chop.

3. In a medium bowl, combine the shrimp, scallions, water chestnuts, wine, oil, ginger and salt. Stir in the cornstarch and egg white. Add the peanuts, tomatoes and cilantro; stir to combine.

4. Place the chard leaves on a clean, dry work surface. Spoon 2 tablespoons of the shrimp mixture onto each chard leaf; fold in the ends and roll up jelly-roll fashion.

5. In a large saucepan, bring 2" of water to a boil. Arrange the chard rolls on a steamer rack; place in the saucepan and cover with a tight-fitting lid. Reduce the heat and steam until cooked through, about 7 minutes.

Oven-Fried Spring Rolls

makes 4 servings

one pot

rush hour

vegetarian

Serving provides:
1 Bread, 1 Fruit/
Vegetable, 1 Fat.

Per serving:
178 Calories,
5 g Total Fat,
1 g Saturated Fat,
3 mg Cholesterol,
749 mg Sodium,
28 g Total
Carbohydrate,
3 g Dietary Fiber,
6 g Protein,
47 mg Calcium.

Points per serving: 3.

Make sure you use Asian sesame oil—it's made from toasted sesame seeds, so it's quite dark. With its rich flavor, you'll never guess that these spring rolls are baked, not deep-fried.

2 tablespoons reduced-sodium soy sauce

2 teaspoons grated peeled gingerroot

½ teaspoon firmly packed light brown sugar

½ teaspoon salt

1 carrot, shredded

1 red bell pepper, seeded and julienned

1 green bell pepper, seeded and julienned

1 cup trimmed snow peas, julienned

1 cup bean sprouts

Four 7"-square egg roll wrappers

4 teaspoons Asian sesame oil

4 teaspoons hot Chinese mustard (optional)

1. Preheat the oven to 400° F. Spray a nonstick baking sheet with nonstick cooking spray, or line a baking sheet with parchment.

2. In a large bowl, combine the soy sauce, ginger, brown sugar and salt. Add the carrot, bell peppers, snow peas and bean sprouts; toss to coat.

3. Place the egg roll wrappers on a clean, dry work surface. Divide the mixture evenly among the wrappers; fold in the ends and roll up jelly-roll fashion. Brush each spring roll with 1 teaspoon of the oil and place on the prepared baking sheet. Bake until the spring rolls are crisp on the bottoms, about 7 minutes; turn and bake until crisp all over, about 5 minutes. Serve with the mustard (if desired).

Steamed Beef Rolls

makes 4 servings

With their meaty texture and flavor, shiitake mushrooms really bring out the flavor of the beef—you need only a small amount.

2 tablespoons reduced-sodium
    soy sauce

4 teaspoons Asian sesame oil

1 tablespoon honey

2 teaspoons fresh lime juice

¼ teaspoon salt

5 ounces sirloin tip, cut into ¼" strips

2 cups sliced shiitake mushrooms

1 cup trimmed snow peas, cut into
    ¼" strips

1 cup bean sprouts

½ red bell pepper, seeded and minced

Four 7"-square egg-roll wrappers

1. In a large bowl, combine the soy sauce, oil, honey, lime juice and salt. Add the beef and toss to coat. Stir in the mushrooms, snow peas, bean sprouts and pepper.

2. Place the egg-roll wrappers on a clean, dry work surface. Divide the beef mixture evenly among the wrappers; fold in the ends and roll up jelly-roll fashion.

3. In a large saucepan, bring 2" of water to a boil. Arrange the beef rolls on a steamer rack; place in the saucepan and cover with a tight-fitting lid. Reduce the heat and steam until cooked through, about 7 minutes.

one pot

rush hour

Serving provides:
1 Bread, 1 Fruit/
Vegetable, 1 Protein/
Milk, 1 Fat.

Per serving:
219 Calories,
6 g Total Fat,
1 g Saturated Fat,
22 mg Cholesterol,
463 mg Sodium,
29 g Total
Carbohydrate,
2 g Dietary Fiber,
12 g Protein,
30 mg Calcium.

Points per serving: 5.

Vegetable and Pork Wontons

makes 4 servings

Fresh wonton skins can be found in the produce department. They'll keep up to 5 days, stored in plastic wrap in the refrigerator.

½ pound trimmed lean pork loin, cut into 1" chunks

1 egg

4 scallions, minced

¼ red bell pepper, seeded and minced

2 teaspoons Asian sesame oil

¾ teaspoon ground ginger

½ teaspoon salt

Twenty 3"-square wonton skins

2 tablespoons rice vinegar

4 teaspoons reduced-sodium soy sauce

1 teaspoon sugar

1. In a food processor, finely grind the pork. Transfer to a medium bowl; stir in the egg, scallions, pepper, oil, ginger and salt.

2. Place the wonton skins on a clean, dry work surface. Spoon 1 generous tablespoon of the pork mixture into the center of each wonton skin. Brush the edges of each wonton skin with water and fold over horizontally to seal, pressing the edges.

3. In a large saucepan, bring 2" of water to a boil. Arrange the wontons on a steamer rack; place in the saucepan and cover with a tight-fitting lid. Reduce the heat and steam, until cooked through, about 7 minutes.

4. Meanwhile, in a small skillet over medium-high heat, bring the vinegar, soy sauce, sugar and 1 tablespoon water to a boil. When ready to serve, spoon the sauce over the wontons.

Spicy Chicken Dumplings with Cilantro and Peanuts

makes 4 servings

one pot

rush hour

spicy

Serving provides:
1 Bread, 1 Fruit/
Vegetable, 1 Protein/
Milk, 1 Fat.

Per serving:
212 Calories,
5 g Total Fat,
1 g Saturated Fat,
32 mg Cholesterol,
534 mg Sodium,
24 g Total
Carbohydrate,
2 g Dietary Fiber,
18 g Protein,
53 mg Calcium.

Points per serving: 4.

Cilantro is a love-it-or-leave-it flavor. If you can leave it, use flat-leaf parsley in its place.

½ pound ground skinless chicken breast

16 scallions, minced

½ cup minced cilantro

¼ cup unsalted dry-roasted peanuts, coarsely chopped

1 egg white

½ teaspoon salt

½ teaspoon ground ginger

¼ teaspoon hot red pepper sauce

Twenty 3"-round wonton skins

1. In a medium bowl, combine the chicken, scallions, cilantro, peanuts, egg white, salt, ginger and pepper sauce.

2. Place the wonton skins on a clean, dry work surface. Spoon 1 scant tablespoon of the filling into the center of each wonton skin. Brush one-half of the edge of each wonton skin with water and fold over to seal, pressing the edges.

3. In a large saucepan, bring 2" of water to a boil. Arrange the dumplings on a steamer rack; place in the saucepan and cover with a tight-fitting lid. Reduce the heat and steam until cooked through, about 7 minutes.

Steamed Shrimp and Pork Dumplings

makes 4 servings

one pot

rush hour

Serving provides:
1 Bread, 2 Protein/
Milks.

Per serving:
215 Calories,
4 g Total Fat,
1 g Saturated Fat,
70 mg Cholesterol,
448 mg Sodium,
25 g Total
Carbohydrate,
1 g Dietary Fiber,
18 g Protein,
50 mg Calcium.

Points per serving: 4.

Round wonton skins are from northern China; they're usually made from flour and water (square wrappers are from Canton in southern China and have egg added). Round wonton skins aren't as delicate as are the square ones, so they're used for chunkier fillings.

¼ pound large shrimp, peeled, deveined and coarsely chopped

¼ pound lean ground pork

8 scallions, minced

½ cup minced cilantro

¼ red bell pepper, seeded and minced

¼ carrot, minced

2 tablespoons seltzer or club soda

1 tablespoon reduced-sodium soy sauce

1 tablespoon rice wine or dry sherry

1 egg white

¼ teaspoon hot red pepper sauce

1 tablespoon cornstarch

Twenty 3"-round wonton skins

1. In a medium bowl, combine the shrimp, pork, scallions, cilantro, bell pepper, carrot, seltzer, soy sauce, wine, egg white and pepper sauce. Stir in the cornstarch.

2. Place the wonton skins on a clean, dry work surface. Spoon 1 generous tablespoon of the shrimp mixture into the center of each wonton skin. Brush one-half of the edge of each wonton skin with water and fold over to seal, pressing the edges.

3. In a large saucepan, bring 2" of water to a boil. Arrange the dumplings on a steamer rack; place in the saucepan and cover with a tight-fitting lid. Reduce the heat and steam until cooked through, about 7 minutes.

Vegetable Dumpling "Logs" with Peanut Sauce

makes 4 servings

Square wonton skins, with their added egg, are a deeper yellow than are the round skins. They are thinner and softer as well; handle them gently.

2 leeks, cleaned and julienned

1 carrot, julienned

1 red bell pepper, seeded and julienned

3 teaspoons Asian sesame oil

1 teaspoon sugar

½ teaspoon salt

Twenty 3"-square wonton skins

2 tablespoons minced cilantro

1 tablespoon rice vinegar

1 tablespoon reduced-sodium soy sauce

1 tablespoon creamy peanut butter

⅛ teaspoon hot red pepper sauce

rush hour

vegetarian

Serving provides:
1 Bread, 1 Fruit/
Vegetable, 1 Fat.

Per serving:
210 Calories,
6 g Total Fat,
1 g Saturated Fat,
3 mg Cholesterol,
666 mg Sodium,
34 g Total
Carbohydrate,
3 g Dietary Fiber,
6 g Protein,
59 mg Calcium.

Points per serving: 4.

(See photo insert.)

1. In a medium pot of boiling water, cook the leeks, carrot and pepper about 1 minute; drain, rinse under cold water and drain again. Transfer to a medium bowl; add 2 teaspoons of the oil, ½ teaspoon of the sugar and the salt; toss to coat.

2. Place the wonton skins on a clean, dry work surface. Divide the mixture evenly among the wonton skins. Brush the edges of the wonton skins with water and roll into logs.

3. In a large saucepan, bring 2" of water to a boil. Arrange the logs on a steamer rack; place in the saucepan and cover with a tight-fitting lid. Reduce the heat and steam until the vegetables and wonton skins are tender, about 5 minutes.

4. Meanwhile, in a small bowl, whisk the cilantro, vinegar, soy sauce, peanut butter, pepper sauce, the remaining 1 teaspoon of the oil and the remaining ½ teaspoon of the sugar until smooth. When ready to serve, drizzle the logs evenly with the sauce.

Steamed Vegetable Dumplings

makes 4 servings

With its knobs, gingerroot can be hard to peel. Scrape the side of a spoon across it to remove the skin—it's as effective as a paring knife or a vegetable peeler, and a lot less hazardous.

rush hour

vegetarian

Serving provides:
1 Bread, 1 Fruit/
Vegetable, 1 Fat.

Per serving:
155 Calories,
3 g Total Fat,
0 g Saturated Fat,
3 mg Cholesterol,
265 mg Sodium,
27 g Total
Carbohydrate,
3 g Dietary Fiber,
6 g Protein,
130 mg Calcium.

Points per serving: 3.

2 teaspoons Asian sesame oil

1 tablespoon minced peeled gingerroot

3 garlic cloves, minced

1½ cups thawed frozen chopped spinach, squeezed dry

16 scallions, minced

Twenty 3"-round wonton skins

1. In a large nonstick skillet, heat the oil until it just begins to smoke, 30–40 seconds. Add the ginger and garlic; cook until just fragrant (do not burn), about 15 seconds. Add the spinach and scallions; cook, stirring as needed, until the vegetables are tender-crisp, about 5 minutes.

2. Place the wonton skins on a clean, dry work surface. Spoon 1 generous tablespoon of the spinach mixture into the center of each wonton skin. Brush one-half of the edge of each wonton skin with water and fold over to seal, pressing the edges.

3. In a large saucepan, bring 2" of water to a boil. Arrange the dumplings on a steamer rack; place in the saucepan and cover with a tight-fitting lid. Reduce the heat and steam until tender, about 5 minutes.

Seven Tips for Eating in Chinese Restaurants

1. Steamed vegetable dumplings make a great lunch all by themselves. Tasty, filling and almost fat-free.

2. The teacup in most Chinese restaurants holds exactly half a cup. Use it to measure rice and main-dish portions, or just to eyeball what you're putting on your plate.

3. Words like "creaky" or "crispy" almost always mean "fried." Look for words like "stir-fried" or, a better choice, "steamed."

4. Save yourself a lot of unwanted oil, calories and cornstarch: Ask for your food to be served plain, with the sauce on the side.

5. Drink plenty of tea; the hot liquid helps you feel full.

6. The free fortune cookie at the end of the meal has 50 calories. Think before you eat it: You might prefer to use those calories for something a bit more memorable.

7. Brown rice has more fiber and nutrients than does white rice. It also has more flavor.

Salmon Pot Stickers with Sweet-and-Sour Dipping Sauce

makes 4 servings

A good nonstick pan is essential for making these delicious dumplings—otherwise, they might stick to the pot! Don't discard the calcium-rich salmon bones—just mash them in.

Dipping Sauce:

1 tablespoon reduced-sodium soy sauce

1 tablespoon rice vinegar

1 scallion, thinly sliced

½ teaspoon sugar

Dumplings:

½ cup canned red salmon

¼ carrot, shredded

2 scallions, thinly sliced

2 tablespoons chopped water chestnuts

½ teaspoon grated peeled gingerroot

½ teaspoon reduced-sodium soy sauce

½ teaspoon rice vinegar

Sixteen 3"-round wonton skins

2 teaspoons peanut oil

one pot

Serving provides:
1 Bread, 1 Fat.

Per serving:
137 Calories,
4 g Total Fat,
1 g Saturated Fat,
9 mg Cholesterol,
522 mg Sodium,
19 g Total
Carbohydrate,
1 g Dietary Fiber,
6 g Protein,
54 mg Calcium.

Points per serving: 3.

1. To prepare the dipping sauce, in a small bowl, combine the soy sauce, vinegar, scallion and sugar with 2 tablespoons water.

2. Remove and discard any skin from the salmon. With a fork, mash the salmon and any bones into tiny pieces. Stir in the carrot, scallions, water chestnuts, ginger, soy sauce and vinegar.

3. Place the wonton skins on a clean, dry work surface. Spoon 1 teaspoon of the salmon mixture into the center of each wonton skin. Brush one-half of the edge of each wonton skin with water and fold over to seal, pressing the edges.

4. In a large nonstick skillet, heat 1 teaspoon of the oil, shaking the skillet to coat evenly. Add eight of the pot stickers and cook, shaking the skillet occasionally, until they are lightly browned on bottom, about 2 minutes. Turn over and cook 1 minute longer. Add enough water to cover the pot stickers halfway. Reduce the heat and simmer, turning the pot stickers occasionally, until cooked through and the liquid is evaporated, 4–5 minutes. Transfer to a plate and keep warm. Wipe out the skillet with a paper towel and repeat with the remaining oil and pot stickers. Serve with the dipping sauce.

chapter 4

STIR-FRIES

Spicy Tangerine Beef

makes 4 servings

Try this Szechuan specialty over rice or noodles. For a more potent tangerine flavor, look for dried tangerine rind in an Asian grocery store. To substitute the dried rind for the fresh zest used in the recipe, soak 4–5 strips in warm water until soft, then slice them into slivers.

one pot

make ahead

Serving provides:
1 Protein/Milk, 1 Fat.

Per serving:
162 Calories,
6 g Total Fat,
2 g Saturated Fat,
33 mg Cholesterol,
239 mg Sodium,
9 g Total Carbohydrate, 2 g Dietary
Fiber, 15 g Protein,
39 mg Calcium.

Points per serving: 3.

1 tablespoon reduced-sodium soy sauce

1 tablespoon rice wine or dry sherry

2 teaspoons hoisin sauce

1 teaspoon Asian sesame oil

½ teaspoon minced peeled gingerroot

½ pound beef round or sirloin, trimmed and cut into thin 2" strips

2 teaspoons peanut oil

2 dried Szechuan chile peppers,* seeds removed and discarded

Slivered zest of 1 small tangerine

2 cups trimmed snow peas, steamed

1 teaspoon cornstarch, dissolved in 2 tablespoons water

1. To prepare the marinade, in a gallon-size sealable plastic bag, combine the soy sauce, wine, hoisin sauce, sesame oil and ginger; add the beef. Seal the bag, squeezing out the air; turn to coat the beef. Refrigerate at least 1 hour, turning the bag occasionally. Drain the beef, reserving the marinade.

2. In a large nonstick skillet or wok, heat 1 teaspoon of the peanut oil. Add the beef and cook, stirring as needed, until barely pink, 1–2 minutes. Transfer the beef and the pan juices to a plate and keep warm. Wipe out the skillet with a paper towel.

3. Return the skillet to the heat, and heat the remaining 1 teaspoon of the peanut oil. Add the peppers and cook, stirring as needed, until blackened, about 1 minute. Add the tangerine zest and cook about 30 seconds. Add the snow peas, the beef, pan juices and the marinade; cook, stirring gently, about 2 minutes. Add the dissolved cornstarch and cook, stirring gently, until the sauce thickens and coats the beef, about 1 minute; serve at once.

See Glossary, page 133.

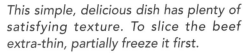

Crispy Beef with Water Chestnuts

makes 4 servings

This simple, delicious dish has plenty of satisfying texture. To slice the beef extra-thin, partially freeze it first.

10 ounces flank steak, trimmed

1 tablespoon reduced-sodium soy sauce

2 teaspoons cornstarch

2 teaspoons peanut oil

8 scallions, thinly sliced

½ red bell pepper, seeded and thinly sliced

¾ cup water chestnuts, sliced

2 tablespoons low-sodium beef broth

1 tablespoon rice wine or dry sherry

1. In a medium bowl, combine the steak, soy sauce and cornstarch; toss to coat.

2. In a large nonstick skillet or wok, heat 1 teaspoon of the oil. Add the scallions and pepper; cook, stirring as needed, until the pepper is softened, about 5 minutes. Transfer to a plate and keep warm.

3. Return the skillet to the heat, and heat the remaining 1 teaspoon of the oil. Add the beef mixture and cook, tossing lightly, until just cooked through, 45–60 seconds. Stir in the vegetables, the water chestnuts, broth and wine; cook, stirring gently, about 2 minutes, until heated through; serve at once.

one pot

rush hour

Serving provides:
2 Protein/Milks,
1 Fat.

Per serving:
174 Calories,
8 g Total Fat,
3 g Saturated Fat,
35 mg Cholesterol,
210 mg Sodium,
9 g Total Carbohy-
drate, 1 g Dietary
Fiber, 15 g Protein,
18 mg Calcium.

Points per serving: 4.

Stir-Fry Smarts

Stir-frying is one of the easiest cooking techniques to master, but there's an art to doing it well. Properly done, stir-fried foods are cooked quickly, using a bare minimum of oil. Follow these steps and you'll get results like a pro.

1. To ensure everything cooks quickly and evenly, cut the ingredients into small, equal-size pieces. Have all of them prepared and ready; place them near the wok, so you can assemble the dish quickly.

2. Items that need partial cooking, like broccoli or carrots, should be steamed until tender-crisp before adding them to the wok; otherwise they'll absorb too much oil before they're fully cooked.

3. Heat the wok until it's very hot *before* adding the oil. (A hot wok heats the oil more evenly, preventing food from sticking to the wok.) Test by sprinkling a few drops of water in the wok; they should sputter and evaporate quickly. Then add the oil and swirl it around the wok to cover the surface evenly.

4. Add the food and seasonings to the hot oil as directed in the recipe, tossing quickly and gently with a wide spatula, a shovel (see page 104) or chopsticks. Keep the food constantly in motion, so that the oil coats it completely and it doesn't stick to the wok.

Ginger Beef and Asparagus Stir-Fry

makes 4 servings

The clean, sharp taste of ginger dominates in this simple yet tasty dish. When you want to wake up everyone's taste buds, serve it with a batch of rice on the side.

make ahead

one pot

Serving provides:
1 Fruit/Vegetable,
1 Protein/Milk, 1 Fat.

Per serving:
154 Calories,
5 g Total Fat,
1 g Saturated Fat,
33 mg Cholesterol,
198 mg Sodium,
10 g Total
Carbohydrate,
2 g Dietary Fiber,
15 g Protein,
41 mg Calcium.

Points per serving: 3.

2 tablespoons rice wine or dry sherry

1 tablespoon reduced-sodium soy sauce

One 1" piece peeled gingerroot, minced

1 garlic clove, minced

½ pound beef round or sirloin, trimmed and cut into thin 2" strips

2 teaspoons peanut oil

1 leek, trimmed, cleaned and thinly sliced

½ teaspoon hot chili paste* (optional)

18 asparagus spears, cut into 3" pieces and steamed

1 carrot, julienned and steamed until tender-crisp

1 teaspoon cornstarch, dissolved in 1 tablespoon water

1. To prepare the marinade, in a gallon-size sealable plastic bag, combine the wine, soy sauce, ginger and garlic; add the beef. Seal the bag, squeezing out the air; turn to coat the beef. Refrigerate at least 1 hour, turning the bag occasionally. Drain the beef, reserving the marinade.

2. In a large nonstick skillet or wok, heat 1 teaspoon of the oil. Add the beef and cook, stirring as needed, until cooked through, 3–4 minutes. Transfer the beef and the pan juices to a plate. Wipe out the skillet with a paper towel.

3. Return the skillet to the heat, and heat the remaining 1 teaspoon of the oil. Add the leek and cook, stirring as needed, until softened, 4–5 minutes. Stir in the chili paste (if using) and cook about 5 seconds longer. Stir in the beef and pan juices, the marinade, asparagus, carrot and the dissolved cornstarch; cook, stirring gently, until the sauce thickens and coats the beef, about 2 minutes; serve at once.

*See Glossary, page 133.

Dry-Cooked Shredded Beef

makes 4 servings

make ahead

one pot

spicy

Serving provides:
1 Fruit/Vegetable,
1 Protein/Milk, 1 Fat.

Per serving:
168 Calories,
8 g Total Fat,
2 g Saturated Fat,
33 mg Cholesterol,
227 mg Sodium,
11 g Total
Carbohydrate,
2 g Dietary Fiber,
15 g Protein,
34 mg Calcium.

Points per serving: 4.

The Szechuan technique of dry-cooking calls for deep-frying in very hot oil; our version succeeds without a lot of oil. Serve with noodles for a complete meal. To make slicing the beef easier, partially freeze it first.

1 tablespoon reduced-sodium soy sauce

1 teaspoon rice vinegar

1 teaspoon Asian sesame oil

½ pound beef round or sirloin, trimmed and cut into thin 2" strips

¼ cup low-sodium chicken broth

1 teaspoon cornstarch

1 teaspoon Worcestershire sauce

1 teaspoon honey

Pinch crushed red pepper flakes

3 teaspoons peanut oil

2 scallions, minced

1 garlic clove, minced

½ teaspoon minced peeled gingerroot

½ teaspoon hot chili paste* (optional)

2 carrots, shredded

1 cup thinly sliced green cabbage

1 cup bean sprouts

1 tablespoon minced cilantro

1. To prepare the marinade, in a gallon-size sealable plastic bag, combine the soy sauce, vinegar and sesame oil; add the beef. Seal the bag, squeezing out the air; turn to coat the beef. Refrigerate at least 30 minutes, turning the bag occasionally. Drain the beef, reserving the marinade. Pat the beef dry with a paper towel.

2. In a small bowl, whisk the broth, cornstarch, Worcestershire sauce, honey and pepper flakes (if using) until smooth.

3. In a large nonstick skillet or wok, heat 2 teaspoons of the peanut oil, until it just begins to smoke, 30–40 seconds. Add the beef; cook, tossing lightly, until lightly browned on the edges, 2–3 minutes. Transfer the beef and the pan juices to a plate and keep warm. Wipe out the skillet with a paper towel.

4. Return the skillet to the heat, and heat the remaining 1 teaspoon of the peanut oil. Add the scallions, garlic and ginger; cook, stirring as needed, until the scallions are softened, 1–2 minutes. Add the chili paste (if using) and cook 5 seconds longer. Stir in the carrots, cabbage and bean sprouts; stir-fry until the carrots are

See Glossary, page 133.

softened, 2–3 minutes. Add the marinade and the broth mixture; cook until the sauce is slightly thickened, 1–2 minutes.

Stir in the beef and cook, stirring gently, until heated through, 1–2 minutes. Sprinkle with the cilantro; serve at once.

Shredded Pork and Bok Choy Stir-Fry

makes 4 servings

Daikon radish gives this tempting stir-fried dish a little pungency. You can also substitute salted daikon radish, available in the fresh vegetable section of some Asian markets; just rinse it first to remove the extra salt.

1 tablespoon reduced-sodium soy sauce

2 teaspoons rice vinegar

2 teaspoons hoisin sauce

1 teaspoon cornstarch

1 teaspoon peanut oil

2 scallions, minced

2 tablespoons grated daikon radish*

1 garlic clove, minced

1 cup sliced shiitake mushrooms

2 cups thinly sliced bok choy (Chinese cabbage)

2 carrots, shredded

1 cup bean sprouts

1 cup shredded cooked lean pork

1. In a small bowl, whisk the soy sauce, vinegar, hoisin sauce and cornstarch with ¼ cup water until smooth.

2. In a large nonstick skillet or wok, heat the oil. Add the scallions, radish and garlic; cook, stirring, until just fragrant, 20–30 seconds. Add the mushrooms; stir-fry until the mushrooms have released and reabsorbed their liquid, 4–5 minutes. Stir in the bok choy, carrots and bean sprouts; cook, stirring as needed, until the bok choy is softened, 4–5 minutes. Add the soy sauce mixture and the pork; cook, stirring gently, until the sauce thickens and coats the pork, 2–3 minutes; serve at once.

one pot

rush hour

Serving provides:
2 Fruit/Vegetables,
1 Protein/Milk.

Per serving:
123 Calories,
4 g Total Fat,
1 g Saturated Fat,
23 mg Cholesterol,
261 mg Sodium,
11 g Total Carbohydrate,
3 g Dietary Fiber,
11 g Protein,
65 mg Calcium.

Points per serving: 2.

*See Glossary, page 133.

"Finely Shredded": How To Do It

There is an economical and healthful reason that many stir-fried dishes call for finely shredded meats and vegetables: Small pieces cook quickly in just a little amount of oil. Fine-tune your shredding finesse with the following technique:

1. With one hand, hold the food firmly on a cutting board; turn your fingers under for safety. Allow your knuckles to act as a guide for the blade as you slowly slice the food straight down into very thin slices. The tip of the blade should remain resting on the cutting board as you slowly lift the blade's other end to cut the food.

2. Slice meat against the grain to break up any fibers, thus making it more tender when cooked. To save time, pile several slices of meat and cut lengthwise into fine strips.

A final tip: Meat and chicken breasts are easier to shred if they are first placed in the freezer for about 20 minutes.

Pork and Black Bean Stir-Fry

makes 4 servings

The secret to this delicious dish is Chinese fermented black beans, available in Asian grocery stores. They'll keep indefinitely, and just a few add a whole lot of flavor. A bowl of steamed brown or white rice is a natural accompaniment.

1 tablespoon reduced-sodium soy sauce

1 teaspoon Asian sesame oil

½ teaspoon minced peeled gingerroot

¼ teaspoon five-spice powder*

½ pound lean pork loin, trimmed and cut into thin 2" strips

2 teaspoons peanut oil

2 scallions, minced

1 tablespoon fermented black beans,* rinsed, drained and finely chopped

1 garlic clove, minced

2 cups sliced mushrooms

2 leeks, cleaned and thinly sliced

1 red bell pepper, seeded and cut into thin strips

1 teaspoon cornstarch, dissolved in ⅓ cup water

1. To prepare the marinade, in a gallon-size sealable plastic bag, combine the soy sauce, sesame oil, ginger and five-spice powder; add the pork. Seal the bag, squeezing out the air; turn to coat the pork. Refrigerate at least 1 hour, turning the bag occasionally. Drain the pork, reserving the marinade.

2. In a large nonstick skillet or wok, heat 1 teaspoon of the peanut oil. Add the pork; cook, stirring as needed, until just cooked through, 3–4 minutes. Transfer the pork and some of the pan juices to a plate and keep warm. Wipe out the skillet with a paper towel.

3. Return the skillet to the heat, and heat the remaining 1 teaspoon of the peanut oil. Add the scallions, black beans and garlic; cook, stirring, until just fragrant, about 15 seconds. Add the mushrooms, leeks and pepper; cook, stirring as needed, until the mushrooms have released and reabsorbed their liquid and the pepper is softened, 4–5 minutes. Stir in the pork, marinade and dissolved cornstarch; cook until the sauce thickens and coats the pork, about 1 minute; serve at once.

make ahead

one pot

Serving provides:
1 Fruit/Vegetable,
1 Protein/Milk, 1 Fat.

Per serving:
168 Calories,
7 g Total Fat,
2 g Saturated Fat,
33 mg Cholesterol,
301 mg Sodium,
12 g Total
Carbohydrate,
2 g Dietary Fiber,
14 g Protein,
51 mg Calcium.

Points per serving: 4.

*See Glossary, page 133.

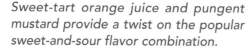

Pork with Orange-Mustard Sauce

makes 4 servings

Sweet-tart orange juice and pungent mustard provide a twist on the popular sweet-and-sour flavor combination.

4 teaspoons vegetable oil

1 pound lean pork loin, trimmed and cut into 4 equal pieces

½ cup low-sodium chicken broth

¼ cup orange juice

⅛ teaspoon salt

⅛ teaspoon freshly ground black pepper

2 teaspoons Dijon mustard

1 cup orange, peeled and sectioned

1 tablespoon minced cilantro

1. In a medium nonstick skillet, heat the oil. Add the pork and cook, turning once, until the outside is browned, about 2 minutes. Reduce the heat and cook, turning once, until no longer pink and cooked through, 4–6 minutes. Transfer the pork to a plate.

2. Add the broth, orange juice, salt and pepper to the skillet; whisk in the mustard. Return the pork to the skillet; add the orange sections and cilantro and cook until heated through, 3–4 minutes.

one pot

rush hour

Serving provides:
1 Fruit/Vegetable,
3 Protein/Milks,
1 Fat.

Per serving:
226 Calories,
11 g Total Fat,
3 g Saturated Fat,
63 mg Cholesterol,
199 mg Sodium,
7 g Total Carbohy-
drate, 1 g Dietary
Fiber, 24 g Protein,
41 mg Calcium.

Points per serving: 5.

Ginger-Pork Stir-Fry

makes 4 servings

Mince ginger quickly and easily in a garlic press, or place it between sheets of wax paper and pound with the smooth side of a mallet.

½ cup low-sodium chicken broth

1 tablespoon oyster sauce*

1 teaspoon cornstarch

¼ pound cellophane noodles*

1 tablespoon peanut oil

2 cups trimmed snow peas

1 red bell pepper, seeded and cut into thin strips

1 tablespoon minced peeled gingerroot

1 teaspoon Asian sesame oil

2 cups cubed cooked lean pork

1. In a small bowl, combine the broth, oyster sauce and cornstarch.

2. Place the cellophane noodles in a medium bowl with enough hot water to cover. Let stand until softened, about 10 minutes. Drain and place on serving platter; keep warm.

3. In a large nonstick skillet or wok, heat the peanut oil. Add the snow peas, pepper and ginger; stir-fry until softened, 2–3 minutes. Place on top of the noodles; keep warm.

4. Return the skillet to the heat, and heat the sesame oil. Add the pork and stir-fry until heated through, 1 minute. Add the broth mixture and cook until the sauce thickens and coats the pork, 1–2 minutes. Spoon the pork and sauce over the vegetables and noodles.

one pot

rush hour

Serving provides:
1 Bread, 1 Fruit/ Vegetable, 2 Protein/ Milks, 1 Fat.

Per serving:
281 Calories,
10 g Total Fat,
3 g Saturated Fat,
46 mg Cholesterol,
228 mg Sodium,
27 g Total Carbohydrate,
3 g Dietary Fiber,
19 g Protein,
52 mg Calcium.

Points per serving: 6.

*See Glossary, page 133.

Kung Pao Chicken

makes 4 servings

make ahead

one pot

spicy

Serving provides:
1 Fruit/Vegetable,
2 Protein/Milks,
1 Fat.

Per serving:
195 Calories,
7 g Total Fat,
1 g Saturated Fat,
37 mg Cholesterol,
309 mg Sodium,
13 g Total
Carbohydrate,
4 g Dietary Fiber,
21 g Protein,
58 mg Calcium.

Points per serving: 4.

Named for Kung Pao Ting, a Chinese nobleman who fled to the Szechuan province during the Ching Dynasty, this classic dish exemplifies the hot and spicy flavors of his adopted homeland.

1 egg white

2 teaspoons cornstarch

Pinch salt

½ pound skinless boneless chicken breasts, cut into ¾" cubes

1 tablespoon hoisin sauce

1 tablespoon rice vinegar

2 teaspoons reduced-sodium soy sauce

1 teaspoon sugar

½ teaspoon hot chili paste*

1 garlic clove, minced

2 teaspoons peanut oil

4 dried Szechuan chile peppers,* seeds removed and discarded

3 cups steamed broccoli florets

¼ cup unsalted dry-roasted peanuts, coarsely chopped

1. In a medium bowl, whisk the egg white, cornstarch and salt until smooth; add the chicken and stir to coat. Refrigerate, covered, about 30 minutes.

2. In a small bowl, combine the hoisin sauce, vinegar, soy sauce, sugar, chili paste and garlic with 3 tablespoons water.

3. In a large nonstick skillet or wok, heat the oil. Add the peppers and cook, stirring as needed, until blackened, about 1 minute. With a slotted spoon, transfer the peppers to a plate, reserving the oil in the skillet.

4. Return the skillet to the heat; add the chicken mixture. Cook, tossing lightly, until the chicken becomes translucent (do not brown), 1–2 minutes. Transfer the chicken and pan juices to a plate and keep warm.

5. Return the skillet to the heat; add the hoisin sauce mixture and cook, stirring constantly, about 30 seconds. Stir in the chicken, the broccoli and peppers; cook, stirring gently, until heated through, 2–3 minutes. Sprinkle with the peanuts; serve at once.

See Glossary, page 133.

Chicken-Spinach Stir-Fry

makes 2 servings

This is an easy and delicious way to include more vegetables in your diet. Serve it over a bed of brown rice.

1 tablespoon reduced-sodium soy sauce

2 teaspoons cornstarch

2 teaspoons rice wine or dry sherry

½ teaspoon honey

¼ teaspoon ground ginger

⅛ teaspoon ground nutmeg

¼ pound skinless boneless chicken breast, cut into strips

1 teaspoon peanut oil

1 celery stalk, thinly sliced

4 cups torn cleaned spinach

make ahead

one pot

Serving provides:
2 Fruit/Vegetables,
2 Protein/Milks,
1 Fat.

Per serving:
153 Calories,
4 g Total Fat,
1 g Saturated Fat,
41 mg Cholesterol,
448 mg Sodium,
10 g Total
Carbohydrate,
3 g Dietary Fiber,
20 g Protein,
127 mg Calcium.

Points per serving: 3.

1. To prepare the marinade, in a quart-size sealable plastic bag, combine the soy sauce, cornstarch, wine, honey, ginger and nutmeg with 1 tablespoon water; add the chicken. Seal the bag, squeezing out the air; turn to coat the chicken. Refrigerate 1 hour, turning the bag occasionally.

2. In a large nonstick skillet or wok, heat the oil. Add the chicken and marinade and cook, stirring constantly, until the chicken is lightly colored and the marinade is boiling, about 3 minutes. Add the celery and cook, stirring constantly, 1 minute longer. Stir in the spinach and stir-fry until the spinach is wilted and the celery is softened, 2–3 minutes; serve at once.

Pang Pang Chicken

makes 4 servings

The components of this delightful cold dish can be prepared in advance and assembled later for a quick supper or picnic.

½ cup low-sodium chicken broth

¼ cup rice wine or dry sherry

One ½" piece peeled gingerroot

½ pound skinless boneless chicken breast

2 cucumbers, peeled, halved lengthwise, seeded and thinly sliced

1 teaspoon salt

1 cup bean sprouts

½ carrot, shredded

1 tablespoon + 1 teaspoon rice vinegar

2 ounces cellophane noodles*

1 teaspoon Asian sesame oil

2 tablespoons natural peanut butter

1 tablespoon reduced-sodium soy sauce

½ teaspoon hot chili paste*

½ teaspoon minced peeled gingerroot

1 garlic clove, minced

2 scallions, minced

1. To prepare the chicken, in a medium saucepan, combine the broth, wine and the ½" piece ginger; bring to a boil. Add the chicken; reduce the heat and simmer, covered, until the chicken is no longer pink, 12–15 minutes. Transfer the chicken to a plate and let cool, then shred with a fork. Discard the ginger and reserve the cooking liquid.

2. To prepare the vegetables and noodles, layer the cucumber slices in a colander, sprinkling with the salt between each layer. Let stand in the sink about 20 minutes to drain, then rinse and pat dry with a paper towel.

3. In a small bowl, combine the bean sprouts and carrot with 1 tablespoon of the vinegar.

4. Place the cellophane noodles in a medium bowl with enough hot water to cover. Let stand until softened, about 10 minutes; drain and place on a serving platter. Toss with the sesame oil.

5. To prepare the sauce, in a blender or mini food processor, puree the cooking liquid, peanut butter, soy sauce, the remaining 1 teaspoon of the vinegar, the chili paste, minced ginger and garlic.

6. To assemble, top the noodles with the cucumber slices and carrot mixture, then top with the shredded chicken. Drizzle with the sauce and sprinkle with the scallions.

See Glossary, page 133.

make ahead

one pot

Serving provides:
1 Bread, 1 Fruit/
Vegetable, 2 Protein/
Milks, 1 Fat.

Per serving:
207 Calories,
6 g Total Fat,
1 g Saturated Fat,
33 mg Cholesterol,
535 mg Sodium,
17 g Total
Carbohydrate,
2 g Dietary Fiber,
17 g Protein,
34 mg Calcium.

Points per serving: 4.

Almond Chicken and Asparagus

makes 4 servings

make ahead

one pot

rush hour

Serving provides:
1 Fruit/Vegetable,
2 Protein/Milks,
1 Fat.

Per serving:
202 Calories,
10 g Total Fat,
1 g Saturated Fat,
33 mg Cholesterol,
88 mg Sodium,
10 g Total
Carbohydrate,
3 g Dietary Fiber,
21 g Protein,
73 mg Calcium.

Points per serving: 4.

A crunchy coating of almonds makes this chicken entrée special. Serve it hot or cold.

36 asparagus stalks, cut into 2" lengths and steamed

½ cup almonds, toasted* and finely chopped

1 egg white

1 tablespoon rice wine or dry sherry

2 teaspoons cornstarch

1 teaspoon sugar

Pinch salt

Pinch five-spice powder†

½ pound skinless boneless chicken breast, cut into thin strips

1 teaspoon peanut oil

1 tablespoon finely minced cilantro

1. Arrange the asparagus on a serving platter; keep warm.

2. Place the almonds in a shallow bowl or pie plate.

3. In a small bowl, whisk the egg white, wine, cornstarch, sugar, salt and five-spice powder until smooth; dip each chicken piece into the mixture to coat, then into the almonds to coat.

4. In a large nonstick skillet or wok, heat the oil. Add half the chicken pieces and cook, stirring gently, until the chicken is cooked through and the edges are golden, 2–3 minutes. Place the chicken in a mound on top of the asparagus; keep warm. Repeat with the remaining chicken. Sprinkle with the cilantro; serve at once, or refrigerate for up to 2 days.

---

*To toast the almonds, preheat the oven to 300° F. Spread the almonds in a shallow baking pan; bake, stirring as needed, until golden brown, 10–15 minutes.

†See Glossary, page 133.

Spicy Szechuan Chicken

makes 4 servings

With its complex flavors, this spicy dish is reminiscent of the classic Szechuan chicken—minus a lot of the fat and calories.

make ahead

spicy

Serving provides:
2 Fruit/Vegetables,
2 Protein/Milks,
1 Fat.

Per serving:
152 Calories,
3 g Total Fat,
1 g Saturated Fat,
41 mg Cholesterol,
248 mg Sodium,
11 g Total
Carbohydrate,
1 g Dietary Fiber,
19 g Protein,
101 mg Calcium.

Points per serving: 3.

½ teaspoon Szechuan peppercorns*

1 teaspoon cinnamon

½ teaspoon anise seeds

1 teaspoon sugar

10 ounces skinless boneless chicken breasts, cut into thin strips

2 teaspoons peanut oil

4 scallions, thinly sliced

One ½" piece peeled gingerroot, minced

2 cups thinly sliced mushrooms

4 cups thinly sliced bok choy (Chinese cabbage)

¾ cup water chestnuts, coarsely chopped

1 tablespoon reduced-sodium soy sauce

1. In a small nonstick skillet, toast the peppercorns, shaking the pan, until they begin to smoke, about 1 minute. Crush in a mortar and pestle or a spice grinder. Sift through a fine sieve and discard the shells, reserving the powder.

2. Return the skillet to the heat, and add the cinnamon and anise seeds; toast, stirring constantly, until fragrant and lightly browned (do not burn), 45–60 seconds. Transfer to a heat-resistant plate and let cool.

3. In a gallon-size sealable plastic bag, combine the peppercorn powder, cinnamon mixture and sugar; add the chicken. Seal the bag, squeezing out the air; shake well to coat the chicken. Refrigerate at least 2 hours, turning the bag occasionally.

4. In a large nonstick skillet or wok, heat 1 teaspoon of the oil. Add the chicken and cook, stirring as needed, until no longer pink, 1–2 minutes. Transfer to a plate and set aside.

5. Return the skillet to the heat, and heat the remaining 1 teaspoon of the oil. Add the scallions and ginger; cook, stirring as needed, until the scallions are softened, about 2 minutes. Add the mushrooms and cook, stirring as needed, until the mushrooms have released and reabsorbed their liquid, 3–4 minutes. Add the bok choy and stir-fry until wilted, 3–4 minutes. Add the chicken, water chestnuts and soy sauce; cook, stirring gently, until heated through, 3–4 minutes. Serve at once.

See Glossary, page 133.

Chicken Chow Mein

makes 4 servings

Chow Mein literally means "fried noodles," but there are endless variations on the theme. This version is typical of what you'll find at your favorite Chinese take-out restaurant. Serve it with hot rice on the side.

½ cup low-sodium chicken broth

1 tablespoon cornstarch

1 tablespoon reduced-sodium soy sauce

1 teaspoon sugar

1 teaspoon peanut oil

4 scallions, thinly sliced

One ½" piece peeled gingerroot, minced

1 garlic clove, minced

2 celery stalks, thinly sliced

½ red bell pepper, seeded and diced

1 cup bean sprouts

1½ cups shredded cooked skinless chicken breast

1 cup chow mein noodles

1. In a small bowl, whisk the broth, cornstarch, soy sauce and sugar until smooth.

2. In a large nonstick skillet or wok, heat the oil. Add the scallions, ginger and garlic; cook, stirring as needed, until the scallions are softened, about 2 minutes. Add the celery and pepper; cook, stirring as needed, until softened, about 5 minutes. Stir in the bean sprouts and stir-fry until softened, about 1 minute. Add the chicken and the broth mixture; cook, stirring gently, until the sauce thickens and coats the chicken, 1–2 minutes. Transfer to a serving platter and arrange the chow mein noodles around the edge; serve at once.

one pot

rush hour

Serving provides:
1 Bread, 1 Fruit/ Vegetable, 1 Protein/ Milk, 1 Fat.

Per serving:
173 Calories,
6 g Total Fat,
1 g Saturated Fat,
36 mg Cholesterol,
262 mg Sodium,
14 g Total Carbohydrate,
1 g Dietary Fiber,
16 g Protein,
28 mg Calcium.

Points per serving: 4.

Curried Turkey Stir-Fry

makes 4 servings

Serve this soul-warming curry over rice—or, for a change, with toasted flatbread.

1 tablespoon reduced-sodium soy sauce

1 teaspoon Asian sesame oil

½ pound skinless boneless turkey breast, cut into thin strips

2 teaspoons peanut oil

½ onion, finely diced

1 tablespoon curry powder

3 cups chopped cauliflower florets, steamed

1 carrot, julienned and steamed

1 cup thawed frozen peas

½ cup low-sodium chicken broth

1 teaspoon cornstarch, dissolved in 1 tablespoon water

make ahead

one pot

Serving provides:
1 Bread, 1 Fruit/
Vegetable, 1 Protein/
Milk, 1 Fat.

Per serving:
171 Calories,
5 g Total Fat,
1 g Saturated Fat,
35 mg Cholesterol,
248 mg Sodium,
15 g Total
Carbohydrate,
5 g Dietary Fiber,
19 g Protein,
58 mg Calcium.

Points per serving: 3.

1. To prepare the marinade, in a gallon-size sealable plastic bag, combine the soy sauce and sesame oil; add the turkey. Seal the bag, squeezing out the air; turn to coat the turkey. Refrigerate at least 30 minutes, turning the bag occasionally. Drain the turkey, reserving the marinade.

2. In a large nonstick skillet or wok, heat 1 teaspoon of the peanut oil. Add the turkey; cook, stirring as needed, 3–4 minutes, until no longer pink. Transfer the turkey and pan juices to a plate and keep warm. Wipe out the skillet with a paper towel.

3. Return the skillet to the heat, and heat the remaining 1 teaspoon of the peanut oil. Add the onion and cook, stirring as needed, until softened, about 5 minutes; sprinkle with the curry powder and cook, stirring, about 30 seconds. Add the turkey, cauliflower, carrot, peas, broth, the marinade and dissolved cornstarch; bring to a boil. Reduce the heat and simmer until the sauce thickens and coats the turkey, 1–2 minutes; serve at once.

Sweet-and-Sour Turkey

makes 4 servings

If you love the restaurant classic Sweet-and-Sour Pork, you'll rave about this fresher-tasting, lighter version.

2 tablespoons reduced-sodium soy sauce

1 tablespoon rice wine or dry sherry

10 ounces skinless boneless turkey breast, cut into ¾" cubes

5 dried Chinese black mushroom caps* (about ½ ounce)

¼ cup + 2 tablespoons cornstarch

4 teaspoons peanut oil

1 green bell pepper, seeded and cut into 1" pieces

1 red bell pepper, seeded and cut into 1" pieces

1 carrot, thinly sliced

1 onion, cut into 1" cubes

½ cup drained canned unsweetened pineapple chunks

4 scallions, cut into 1" lengths

2 garlic cloves, peeled and crushed

One ½" piece peeled gingerroot, minced

2 tablespoons sugar

2 tablespoons red wine vinegar

make ahead

Serving provides:
1 Bread, 1 Fruit/ Vegetable, 2 Protein/ Milks, 1 Fat.

Per serving:
256 Calories,
5 g Total Fat,
1 g Saturated Fat,
44 mg Cholesterol,
350 mg Sodium,
32 g Total Carbohydrate,
3 g Dietary Fiber,
19 g Protein,
37 mg Calcium.

Points per serving: 5.

1. In a gallon-size sealable plastic bag, combine 1 tablespoon of the soy sauce and the wine; add the turkey. Seal the bag, squeezing out the air; turn to coat the turkey. Refrigerate about 30 minutes, turning the bag occasionally. Drain the turkey, discarding any marinade.

2. Meanwhile, in a small saucepan, bring 1 cup water to a boil; add the mushrooms, cover and remove from heat. Let stand until softened, about 20 minutes. Drain, discarding the liquid, and thinly slice.

3. In a small bowl, whisk 1 tablespoon water and 2 teaspoons of the cornstarch until smooth.

4. Sprinkle the remaining cornstarch onto a large sheet of wax paper. Dredge the turkey in the cornstarch, one piece at a time, shaking off the excess, until coated on all sides. Discard any leftover cornstarch.

5. In a large nonstick skillet or wok, heat 1 teaspoon of the oil. Add one-half the turkey and cook, stirring gently, until cooked through and the edges are golden, 4–5 minutes. Transfer to a warmed serving platter; keep warm. Repeat with 1 more teaspoon of the oil and the remaining turkey. Wipe out the skillet with a paper towel.

*See Glossary, page 133.

6. Return the skillet to the heat, and heat 1 more teaspoon of the oil. Add the bell peppers, carrot and onion; cook, stirring gently, until the peppers are very tender, 10–12 minutes. Transfer to a plate and keep warm.

7. Return the skillet to the heat, and heat the remaining 1 teaspoon of the oil. Add the mushrooms, the pineapple, scallions, garlic and ginger; cook, stirring gently, until the scallions are softened and the pineapple is lightly browned, 4–5 minutes. Gently stir in the reserved vegetables; remove from heat. Set aside and keep warm.

8. In a small saucepan, combine the sugar, vinegar and the remaining 1 tablespoon of the soy sauce with ¼ cup water; bring to a boil and stir until the sugar dissolves. Stir in the dissolved cornstarch; cook, stirring gently, until the sauce is thickened, about 2 minutes. Pour the sauce over the vegetables in the skillet and bring just to a boil. Remove and discard the garlic, if desired. To serve, pour the vegetable mixture over the turkey; toss gently to combine.

Moo Shu Turkey

makes 4 servings

This restaurant classic takes a lighter twist when it's made with turkey instead of the usual pork. Pita halves make a quick substitute for the traditional pancakes. To make the turkey easier to slice, partially freeze it first.

2 tablespoons reduced-sodium soy
    sauce

1 teaspoon sugar

½ teaspoon Worcestershire sauce

½ pound skinless boneless turkey
    breast, julienned

5 dried Chinese black mushroom caps*
    (about ½ ounce)

½ ounce dried Chinese "tree ear" fungi*

3 teaspoons peanut oil

3 egg whites, lightly beaten

1 cup shredded napa cabbage

½ red bell pepper, seeded and julienned

1 cup bean sprouts

1 tablespoon rice vinegar

4 small pitas, halved lengthwise

2 tablespoons + 2 teaspoons hoisin
    sauce

8 scallions, trimmed and feathered along
    the white parts to make "flowers"

make ahead

Serving provides:
1 Bread, 1 Fruit/
Vegetable, 1 Protein/
Milk, 1 Fat.

Per serving:
254 Calories,
4 g Total Fat,
1 g Saturated Fat,
31 mg Cholesterol,
743 mg Sodium,
33 g Total
Carbohydrate,
3 g Dietary Fiber,
20 g Protein,
67 mg Calcium.

Points per serving: 5.

(See photo insert.)

1. To prepare the marinade, in a quart-size sealable plastic bag, combine 1 tablespoon of the soy sauce, the sugar and Worcestershire sauce; add the turkey. Seal the bag, squeezing out the air; turn to coat the turkey. Refrigerate at least 30 minutes, turning the bag occasionally. Drain the turkey, reserving the marinade.

2. Meanwhile, in a small saucepan, bring 1 cup water to a boil; add the mushrooms and fungi, cover and remove from heat. Let stand until softened, about 20 minutes. Drain, discarding the liquid; thinly slice the mushrooms and cut the fungi into ½" strips.

3. To prepare the turkey filling, in a large nonstick skillet or wok, heat 1 teaspoon of the oil. Add the turkey and cook, stirring as needed, until no longer pink, 2–3 minutes. Transfer the turkey and pan juices to a plate and keep warm. Wipe out the skillet with a paper towel.

4. Return the skillet to the heat, and heat 1 more teaspoon of the oil. Add the egg whites and cook, stirring as needed, until scrambled, about 1 minute. Transfer to a plate and keep warm; wipe out the skillet with a paper towel.

See Glossary, page 133.

5. Return the skillet to the heat, and heat the remaining 1 teaspoon of the oil. Add the cabbage, pepper, the mushrooms and fungi; cook, stirring as needed, until tender, 6–8 minutes. Stir in the bean sprouts, vinegar, the remaining 1 tablespoon of the soy sauce and the marinade; cook 1 minute longer. Stir in the turkey and egg whites; toss gently to combine.

6. To serve, spread each pita half with 1 teaspoon of the hoisin sauce; spoon the turkey mixture into the center and top with a scallion "flower." Roll up the bottom and sides of the pita half to enclose the filling.

Lean Desserts, the Asian Way

Like most people, the Chinese like a sweet treat now and then, yet they don't often have dessert at the end of a meal. Instead, they might enjoy a cookie with tea, or rice pudding or a small pastry in the middle of a special meal—to refresh the palate and provide a contrast to the other dishes being served.

A more traditional way to finish a Chinese meal is also one of the healthiest: fresh fruit. If you're planning a special Chinese dinner, end it with fresh or canned lychees, juicy and fragrant chestnut-size fruit in a hard, red pod—or kumquats, tiny, tart citrus fruits that look like walnut-size oranges. Both are available at Asian grocery stores.

Or try some of the other fruits listed below, all typically served in China. None will strain your calorie budget, so you might even splurge on a fortune cookie (50 calories).

Fruit	Calories
Apple, 1 small	65
Green Grapes, 1 cup	60
Kumquats, 6	70
Lychees, 10 medium	70
Mango, ½ medium	70
Orange, 1 small	65
Peach, 1 medium	40
Pear, 1 small	65
Plums, 2 small	70

Shrimp Egg Fu Yung

makes 4 servings

At restaurants, these savory omelets can be a fat trap, since they're loaded with whole eggs and, frequently, fried meats. When you make them at home, you can control the fat content without losing any of the wonderful flavor. The omelets can be made up to a day ahead, chilled and reheated in a 350° F oven, but the sauce should always be freshly prepared. Serve the omelets with a steaming platter of rice and some sautéed greens.

make ahead

Serving provides:
1 Fruit/Vegetable,
2 Protein/Milks.

Per serving:
174 Calories,
7 g Total Fat,
2 g Saturated Fat,
270 mg Cholesterol,
384 mg Sodium,
7 g Total Carbohy-
drate, 1 g Dietary
Fiber, 21 g Protein,
59 mg Calcium.

Points per serving: 4.

1 teaspoon peanut oil

½ teaspoon minced peeled gingerroot

1 cup sliced shiitake mushrooms

8 scallions, thinly sliced

1 cup bean sprouts

1 tablespoon reduced-sodium soy sauce

1 teaspoon sugar

3 eggs

3 egg whites

¼ pound cooked peeled small shrimp, chopped

¼ cup low-sodium chicken broth

1 tablespoon rice wine or dry sherry

½ teaspoon Worcestershire sauce

1 teaspoon cornstarch

1 tablespoon minced cilantro

1. To prepare the omelets, in a medium nonstick skillet, heat the oil. Add the ginger and cook, stirring, until just fragrant (do not burn), about 15 seconds. Add the mushrooms and scallions; stir-fry until the mushrooms have released and reabsorbed their liquid and the scallions are softened, 8–10 minutes. Stir in the bean sprouts, soy sauce and sugar; cook, stirring as needed, until heated through. Let cool.

2. In a large bowl, beat the eggs and egg whites until frothy; stir in the cooked vegetables and the shrimp.

3. Wipe the skillet with a paper towel. Spray the skillet with nonstick cooking spray; heat. Add one-fourth of the egg mixture, tilting to cover the bottom of the pan. Cook until the underside is set, 45–60 seconds. Turn and cook until lightly browned, 30–45 seconds. Slide the omelet onto a plate and keep warm. Repeat with the remaining egg mixture, spraying the skillet each time with cooking spray. Make 4 omelets.

4. To prepare the sauce, in a medium saucepan, whisk the broth, wine, Worcestershire sauce and cornstarch until smooth. Bring to a boil; cook, stirring as needed, until thickened, 1–2 minutes. When ready to serve, pour the sauce over the omelets and sprinkle with the cilantro.

Shrimp with Lobster Sauce

makes 4 servings

Looking over this recipe, you might wonder, "Where's the lobster?" This classic dish is so named because the shrimp is cooked in the black bean sauce that is traditionally used on lobster. Serve it with plenty of steamed rice and some crisp veggies like snow peas or green beans on the side.

one pot

rush hour

Serving provides:
2 Protein/Milks,
1 Fat.

Per serving:
144 Calories,
4 g Total Fat,
1 g Saturated Fat,
129 mg Cholesterol,
424 mg Sodium,
5 g Total Carbohydrate, 0 g Dietary Fiber, 20 g Protein,
62 mg Calcium.

Points per serving: 3.

2 teaspoons peanut oil

¾ pound medium shrimp, peeled and deveined

1 tablespoon fermented black beans,* rinsed, drained and finely chopped

1 garlic clove, minced

8 scallions, thinly sliced

⅓ cup low-sodium chicken broth

2 teaspoons cornstarch, dissolved in 2 tablespoons water

1 tablespoon rice wine or dry sherry

1 tablespoon reduced-sodium soy sauce

½ teaspoon sugar

2 egg whites, well beaten

1. In a large nonstick skillet or wok, heat 1 teaspoon of the oil. Add the shrimp and cook, stirring as needed, until just opaque, 2–3 minutes. Transfer to a plate and keep warm. Wipe out the skillet with a paper towel.

2. Return the skillet to the heat, and heat the remaining 1 teaspoon of the oil. Add the black beans and garlic; cook, stirring as needed, until just fragrant (do not burn), about 15 seconds. Add the scallions and stir-fry until the scallions are very soft, 5–8 minutes. Stir in the shrimp, the broth, dissolved cornstarch, wine, soy sauce and sugar; bring to a boil and cook, stirring, until the sauce is slightly thickened, about 1 minute. Remove from heat and add the egg whites, pouring in a thin stream around the sides of the skillet. Stir until the egg whites are cooked, about 1 minute; serve at once.

*See Glossary, page 133.

Shrimp Fried Rice

make ahead

one pot

rush hour

Serving provides:
2 Breads, 1 Fruit/
Vegetable, 1 Protein/
Milk, 1 Fat.

Per serving:
267 Calories,
5 g Total Fat,
1 g Saturated Fat,
143 mg Cholesterol,
433 mg Sodium,
33 g Total
Carbohydrate,
2 g Dietary Fiber,
21 g Protein,
67 mg Calcium.

Points per serving: 5.

This tasty, quick entrée is a great crowd pleaser; doubling the recipe makes it easy party fare. Make the rice a day ahead so it's thoroughly chilled when you add it.

1 egg

2 egg whites

2½ cups cold cooked rice

2 teaspoons peanut oil

½ pound small shrimp, peeled

¼ cup diced lean ham

8 scallions, thinly sliced

½ red bell pepper, seeded and diced

½ cup thawed frozen peas

1 cup bean sprouts

1 tablespoon oyster sauce*

1. In a small bowl, whisk the egg and egg whites until frothy.

2. With moistened fingers, stir the rice to separate the grains.

3. In a large nonstick skillet or wok, heat 1 teaspoon of the oil. Add the shrimp and ham; cook, tossing lightly, just until the shrimp turn barely pink, 30 seconds–1 minute. Transfer to a plate and keep warm. Wipe out the skillet with a paper towel.

4. Return the skillet to the heat, and heat the remaining 1 teaspoon of the oil. Add the scallions and pepper; cook, stirring as needed, until softened, about 5 minutes. Add the rice, stirring quickly, and stir-fry until heated through, about 1 minute.

5. Make a well in the center of the rice and add the egg mixture, stirring the eggs constantly, until they are soft-scrambled, about 1 minute. Immediately start incorporating the rice mixture, stirring in a circular motion. When thoroughly blended, add the peas and cook, stirring constantly, 1 minute longer. Add the bean sprouts, the shrimp mixture and the oyster sauce; cook, tossing lightly, until the bean sprouts are tender, about 2 minutes; serve at once.

*See Glossary, page 133.

Shrimp, Pork and Broccoli Stir-Fry

makes 4 servings

Serve this colorful, crunchy stir-fry over a bed of noodles.

1 tablespoon reduced-sodium soy sauce

1 tablespoon rice wine or dry sherry

1 teaspoon minced peeled gingerroot

1 teaspoon hoisin sauce

¼ pound trimmed lean pork, cut into thin strips

½ cup low-sodium chicken broth

2 teaspoons cornstarch

3 teaspoons peanut oil

½ teaspoon hot chili paste*

½ pound medium shrimp, peeled and deveined

4 scallions, thinly sliced

1 garlic clove, minced

2 cups broccoli florets, steamed

2 carrots, julienned and steamed

1. To prepare the marinade, in a gallon-size sealable plastic bag, combine the soy sauce, wine, ginger and hoisin sauce; add the pork. Seal the bag, squeezing out the air; turn to coat the pork. Refrigerate at least 1 hour, turning the bag occasionally. Drain the pork, reserving the marinade.

2. In a small bowl, whisk the broth and cornstarch until smooth.

3. In a large nonstick skillet or wok, heat 1 teaspoon of the oil. Add the chili paste and cook, stirring constantly, about 10 seconds; add the shrimp and cook, stirring as needed, until the shrimp are barely pink, 1–2 minutes. Transfer to a plate and keep warm. Wipe out the skillet with a paper towel.

4. Return the skillet to the heat, and heat 1 more teaspoon of the oil. Add the pork and cook, stirring as needed, until no longer pink, 2–3 minutes. Transfer the pork and pan juices to the plate with the shrimp and keep warm. Wipe out the skillet with a paper towel.

5. Return the skillet to the heat, and heat the remaining 1 teaspoon of the oil. Add the scallions and garlic; cook, stirring as needed, until softened, 3–4 minutes. Stir in the broccoli, carrots and the marinade; bring to a boil and cook, stirring as needed, about 1 minute. Stir in the pork, shrimp and the broth mixture; cook, stirring as needed, until the sauce thickens, 2–3 minutes; serve at once.

See Glossary, page 133.

make ahead

one pot

Serving provides:
1 Fruit/Vegetable,
2 Protein/Milks,
1 Fat.

Per serving:
205 Calories,
7 g Total Fat,
2 g Saturated Fat,
107 mg Cholesterol,
345 mg Sodium,
13 g Total Carbohydrate,
4 g Dietary Fiber,
23 g Protein,
87 mg Calcium.

Points per serving: 4.

Calorie Bargain or Calorie Disaster?

You probably know what to avoid at a Chinese restaurant—anything that the menu describes as fried, breaded, with eggs or nuts, or with the word "crispy" in the name—and that baked, broiled, stir-fried and steamed are the terms to look for. But oh, what a difference those words (and cooking methods!) can make:

Six Calorie Bargains in a Chinese Restaurant

1. 5 Steamed Vegetable Dumplings: 65 calories

2. ⅔ cup Braised Mixed Vegetables: 96 calories

3. 1 cup Egg Drop Soup: 110 calories

4. 9 Clams with Black Bean Sauce: 199 calories

5. 1 cup Broccoli with Beef: 172 calories

6. ¼ pound Shrimp with Garlic Sauce: 260 calories

Six Calorie Disasters in a Chinese Restaurant

1. 6 Barbecued Spare Ribs: 767 calories

2. Moo Shu Pork (2 pancakes): 582 calories

3. 1 cup Kung Pao Chicken: 720 calories

4. 1 cup Sweet-and-Sour Pork: 720 calories

5. 1 cup Hot and Spicy Shredded Beef: 515 calories

6. 1½ cups Cold Noodles with Sesame Sauce: 486 calories

Scallop-Cucumber Stir-Fry

makes 4 servings

make ahead

one pot

Serving provides:
2 Fruit/Vegetables,
2 Protein/Milks,
1 Fat.

Per serving:
209 Calories,
5 g Total Fat,
1 g Saturated Fat,
47 mg Cholesterol,
533 mg Sodium,
14 g Total
Carbohydrate,
2 g Dietary Fiber,
25 g Protein,
68 mg Calcium.

Points per serving: 4.

Soft scallops and crisp cucumbers provide deliciously contrasting textures in this Cantonese-inspired dish.

2 tablespoons rice wine or dry sherry

½ teaspoon minced peeled gingerroot

¼ teaspoon onion powder

1¼ pounds scallops

4 cucumbers, peeled, halved lengthwise, seeded and thinly sliced

1 teaspoon salt

¼ cup low-sodium chicken broth

2 teaspoons cornstarch

1 teaspoon Asian sesame oil

½ teaspoon sugar

2 teaspoons peanut oil

2 carrots, diced and steamed

1. To prepare the marinade, in a gallon-size sealable plastic bag, combine the wine, ginger and onion powder; add the scallops. Seal the bag, squeezing out the air; turn to coat the scallops. Refrigerate at least 30 minutes, turning the bag occasionally. Drain the scallops, reserving the marinade. Pat the scallops dry with a paper towel.

2. Meanwhile, layer the cucumber slices in a colander, sprinkling with the salt between each layer. Let stand in the sink about 20 minutes to drain, then rinse and pat the slices dry with a paper towel.

3. In a small bowl, whisk the broth, cornstarch, sesame oil and sugar until smooth.

4. In a large nonstick skillet or wok, heat 1 teaspoon of the peanut oil. Add the scallops and cook, stirring as needed, until just opaque, 1–2 minutes. Transfer to a plate and keep warm. Wipe out the skillet with a paper towel.

5. Return the skillet to the heat, and heat the remaining 1 teaspoon of the peanut oil. Add the cucumbers, carrots and the marinade; bring to a rolling boil. Reduce the heat; cook, about 2 minutes, tossing lightly. Add the scallops and the broth mixture; cook, stirring as needed, until the sauce thickens and coats the scallops, 1–2 minutes. Serve at once.

Spicy Soft-Shell Crabs

makes 4 servings

one pot

rush hour

spicy

Serving provides:
2 Protein/Milks,
1 Fat.

Per serving:
201 Calories,
6 g Total Fat,
1 g Saturated Fat,
135 mg Cholesterol,
639 mg Sodium,
5 g Total Carbohy-
drate, 0 g Dietary
Fiber, 28 g Protein,
17 mg Calcium.

Points per serving: 5.

Soft-shell crabs, which can indeed be eaten shell and all, are highly perishable; buy them live, have your fishmonger clean them for you, and cook them within 4 hours of purchasing. These tasty morsels used to be a delicacy relegated only to the late spring and early summer, when crabs shed their shells. Nowadays, commercial crab fishery has extended the season, but the dish is still a wonderful way to welcome the warmer weather.

1 tablespoon rice wine or dry sherry

1 tablespoon reduced-sodium soy sauce

1 teaspoon cornstarch

1 teaspoon firmly packed dark brown sugar

4 teaspoons peanut oil

8 small (3-ounce) soft-shell crabs, cleaned

One ½" piece peeled gingerroot, minced

1 garlic clove, minced

8 scallions, cut into 2" lengths

1 tablespoon fermented black beans,* rinsed, drained and finely chopped

1. In a small bowl, whisk the wine, soy sauce, cornstarch, brown sugar and ¼ cup water until smooth.

2. In a large nonstick skillet, heat 1 tablespoon of the oil. Add 4 of the crabs, shell-side down, and cook until their shells turn reddish brown, 1–2 minutes. Turn with a spatula or tongs and cook until browned, 1–2 minutes. Transfer to a plate and keep warm; repeat with the remaining crabs.

3. Return the skillet to the heat, and heat the remaining 1 teaspoon of the oil. Add the ginger and garlic; cook, stirring, until just fragrant (do not burn), about 15 seconds. Add the scallions and black beans; stir-fry until the scallions are softened, 3–4 minutes. Add the crabs and wine mixture; cook, stirring gently, until the sauce thickens and coats the crabs, about 2 minutes. Serve at once.

See Glossary, page 133.

The Well-Tempered Wok

You don't *have* to have a wok to make great Chinese food, but it *is* nice to have something so versatile in the kitchen. Its sloping sides and large cooking surface make stir-frying a breeze, and it can be used for steaming, braising, deep-frying or even smoking foods as well.

Woks work best on a gas stove, since direct flame heats them best, but you can get pretty good results with an electric range if you choose a flat-bottomed wok that sits directly on the burner. Steer clear of electric woks, however; they don't get hot enough to stir-fry properly. Look for iron or steel woks—the heavier the better—and avoid stainless steel or light aluminum ones, which don't heat evenly.

A new wok needs to be "seasoned" before using—in order to create a nonsticking surface. Here's how:

1. Scrub the wok with dishwashing detergent and a stiff brush to remove any coatings added by the manufacturer to prevent rusting in the store. Dry thoroughly.

2. Pour 1½ cups of vegetable oil (peanut, safflower or corn oils are best) into the wok and swirl it around, coating its entire surface.

3. Place the wok over a medium heat and, while gently shaking the pan occasionally to swirl the oil around, heat until the oil begins to smoke. Remove the wok from the heat and let cool.

4. Swirl the cooled oil around again to coat the surface of the wok, return the wok to a medium heat and repeat Step 3 two or three times, until the wok is well-coated. Pour out and discard the oil; wipe out the wok with a paper towel.

5. To clean the wok, scrub with a brush and dishwashing detergent. Rinse and pat dry, then place over a high heat to evaporate any remaining water (and thus prevent rust). If your wok is prone to rusting, spray the surface lightly with nonstick cooking spray and wipe with a paper towel before storing.

Five-Spice Tofu Stir-Fry

make ahead

one pot

spicy

vegetarian

Serving provides:
1 Fruit/Vegetable,
1 Protein/Milk, 1 Fat.

Per serving:
117 Calories,
4 g Total Fat,
1 g Saturated Fat,
0 mg Cholesterol,
372 mg Sodium,
14 g Total
Carbohydrate,
2 g Dietary Fiber,
6 g Protein,
55 mg Calcium.

Points per serving: 2.

Tofu takes on a wonderful, subtly sweet flavor and fragrance in this unusual dish; use light (reduced-fat) tofu if you can find it in your grocery store. Serve with brown or jasmine rice on the side.

½ pound firm reduced-fat tofu

2 tablespoons reduced-sodium soy sauce

1 tablespoon grated tangerine or orange zest

1 tablespoon white vinegar

1 teaspoon five-spice powder*

½ teaspoon hot chili paste*

One 1" piece peeled gingerroot, minced

1 garlic clove, minced

3 teaspoons peanut oil

8 scallions, thinly sliced

½ red bell pepper, seeded and cut into 1" pieces

1 cup trimmed snow peas, steamed

¾ cup water chestnuts, sliced

2 teaspoons cornstarch, dissolved in 1 tablespoon water

1. To press the tofu, place it between 2 flat plates. Weight the top plate with a heavy object (try a heavy can or a cast-iron skillet) until the tofu bulges at the sides but does not split. Let stand about 30 minutes, then pour off the water that has accumulated. Cut the tofu into ¾" cubes.

2. To prepare the marinade, in a gallon-size sealable plastic bag, combine the soy sauce, tangerine zest, vinegar, five-spice powder, chili paste, ginger and garlic; add the tofu. Seal the bag, squeezing out the air; turn to coat the tofu. Refrigerate at least 3 hours, turning the bag occasionally. Drain the tofu, reserving the marinade.

3. In a large nonstick skillet or wok, heat 2 teaspoons of the oil. Add the tofu and cook, stirring as needed, until lightly browned, 3–4 minutes. Transfer the tofu to a plate and keep warm. Wipe out the skillet with a paper towel.

4. Return the skillet to the heat, and heat the remaining 1 teaspoon of the oil. Add the scallions and pepper; cook, stirring as needed, until softened, about 5 minutes. Add the snow peas, water chestnuts, the tofu, ⅓ cup water and the marinade; cook, tossing gently, until heated through, about 2 minutes. Add the dissolved cornstarch and cook, stirring gently, about 1 minute, until the sauce thickens and coats the tofu; serve at once.

See Glossary, page 133.

Sweet-and-Sour Tofu

makes 2 servings

one pot

rush hour

vegetarian

Serving provides:
2 Fruit/Vegetables,
2 Protein/Milks,
1 Fat.

Per serving:
265 Calories,
6 g Total Fat,
1 g Saturated Fat,
0 mg Cholesterol,
369 mg Sodium,
44 g Total
Carbohydrate,
5 g Dietary Fiber,
12 g Protein,
90 mg Calcium.

Points per serving: 5.

If you're looking for ways to add more soy foods to your family's diet but are encountering a little reluctance on their part, try this dish. Its sweetness just might give you the opportunity you need.

½ cup drained canned unsweetened
    pineapple chunks
    (reserve ⅓ cup juice)

1 tablespoon ketchup

2 teaspoons cornstarch

2 teaspoons reduced-sodium soy sauce

2 teaspoons white vinegar

½ teaspoon honey

¼ teaspoon ground ginger

2 teaspoons peanut oil

6 ounces firm reduced-fat tofu,
    cut into 1" cubes

1 green bell pepper, seeded and
    cut into 1" pieces

½ red bell pepper, seeded and
    cut into 1" pieces

8 scallions, sliced

½ cup drained rinsed canned
    cannellini beans

1. In a medium bowl, whisk the pineapple juice, ketchup, cornstarch, soy sauce, vinegar, honey and ginger until smooth.

2. In a large nonstick skillet, heat the oil. Add the tofu and cook, stirring as needed, until lightly browned, 3–4 minutes. Add the bell peppers and scallions; cook, stirring constantly, until the vegetables are softened, about 5 minutes. Stir in the pineapple chunks, beans and the juice mixture; cook, stirring constantly, until the sauce thickens and coats the tofu, 3–4 minutes. Serve at once.

Buddha's Delight

makes 4 servings

There are as many variations of this classic vegetarian dish as there are towns in China. This version calls for chewy, meat-like wheat gluten ("seitan"), available in Asian markets and health-food stores.

5 dried Chinese black mushroom caps*
   (about ½ ounce)

½ ounce dried Chinese "tree ear" fungi*

1 tablespoon reduced-sodium soy sauce

2 teaspoons rice vinegar

2 teaspoons hoisin sauce

1 teaspoon cornstarch

2 teaspoons peanut oil

¼ pound wheat gluten,* rinsed and
   thinly sliced

1 garlic clove, minced

½ teaspoon minced peeled gingerroot

8 scallions, thinly sliced

2 cups sliced bok choy

1 carrot, julienned

1 cup drained rinsed canned baby
   corn ears

1 cup bean sprouts

½ cup drained rinsed canned sliced
   bamboo shoots

vegetarian

Serving provides:
2 Fruit/Vegetables,
1 Fat.

Per serving:
132 Calories,
3 g Total Fat,
0 g Saturated Fat,
0 mg Cholesterol,
259 mg Sodium,
19 g Total
Carbohydrate,
6 g Dietary Fiber,
8 g Protein,
93 mg Calcium.

Points per serving: 2.

(See photo insert.)

1. In a small saucepan, bring 1 cup water to a boil. Add the mushrooms and fungi; cover and remove from heat. Let stand until softened, about 20 minutes. Drain, discarding the liquid; thinly slice the mushrooms and cut the fungi into ½" strips.

2. In a small bowl, whisk the soy sauce, vinegar, hoisin sauce, cornstarch and ¼ cup water until smooth.

3. In a large nonstick skillet or wok, heat 1 teaspoon of the oil. Add the wheat gluten and cook, stirring as needed, until lightly browned, 3–4 minutes. Transfer to a plate and keep warm. Wipe out the skillet with a paper towel.

4. Return the skillet to the heat, and heat the remaining 1 teaspoon of the oil. Add the garlic and ginger; cook, stirring as needed, until just fragrant (do not burn), about 15 seconds. Add the scallions and stir-fry until softened, 3–4 minutes. Stir in the bok choy, carrot and ¼ cup water; cook, stirring as needed, until the carrot is tender and most of the liquid is evaporated, 8–10 minutes. Stir in the wheat gluten, baby corn, bean

*See Glossary, page 133.

sprouts, bamboo shoots and the mushrooms and fungi; cook, stirring constantly, 1 minute. Stir in the soy sauce mixture; cook, stirring gently, until the sauce is thickened, about 2 minutes. Serve at once.

. Hot-and-Sour Cabbage

makes 4 servings

one pot

rush hour

vegetarian

Serving provides:
2 Fruit/Vegetables,
1 Fat.

Per serving:
77 Calories,
5 g Total Fat,
1 g Saturated Fat,
0 mg Cholesterol,
179 mg Sodium,
8 g Total Carbohy-
drate, 1 g Dietary
Fiber, 2 g Protein,
96 mg Calcium.

Points per serving: 2.

Try this piquant side dish hot or cold. Either way, it provides a shot of peppery, sour flavor that pairs well with rich dishes. The recipe doubles easily.

2 tablespoons white vinegar

1 tablespoon reduced-sodium soy sauce

2 teaspoons cornstarch

1 teaspoon sugar

3 teaspoons peanut oil

6 cups chopped napa cabbage
    (1" chunks), green and white
    parts separated

1 teaspoon Asian sesame oil

3–4 dried Szechuan chile peppers,*
    seeds removed and discarded

4 scallions, thinly sliced

One ½" piece peeled gingerroot,
    minced

½ teaspoon hot chili paste*

1. In a small bowl, whisk the vinegar, soy sauce, cornstarch and sugar until smooth.

2. In a large nonstick skillet or wok, heat 1 teaspoon of the peanut oil. Add the white cabbage chunks and cook, stirring as needed, until the pieces are thoroughly coated with oil, about 1 minute. Add ¼ cup water; cook 1 minute longer. Stir in the green cabbage chunks and cook, stirring as needed, about 2 minutes longer. Transfer to a medium bowl and toss with the sesame oil. Wipe out the skillet with a paper towel.

3. Return the skillet to the heat, and heat 1 more teaspoon of the peanut oil. Add the peppers and cook, stirring constantly, until blackened, about 1 minute. Add the scallions and ginger; stir-fry until the scallions are softened, 3–4 minutes. Add the chili paste and cook about 5 seconds longer; add the cabbage and stir-fry about 2 minutes. Stir in the vinegar mixture; cook, tossing lightly, until the sauce thickens and coats the cabbage, 2–3 minutes.

See Glossary, page 133.

Dry-Cooked Green Beans

makes 4 servings

one pot

rush hour

vegetarian

Serving provides:
2 Fruit/Vegetables,
1 Fat.

Per serving:
109 Calories,
5 g Total Fat,
1 g Saturated Fat,
0 mg Cholesterol,
161 mg Sodium,
14 g Total
Carbohydrate,
3 g Dietary Fiber,
3 g Protein,
75 mg Calcium.

Points per serving: 2.

Dry-cooking—frying at a high tempera-ture—gives green beans a wonderful texture: slightly crisp on the outside, ten-der and juicy inside. If you have a child who hates vegetables, this dish just might win her over.

1 tablespoon reduced-sodium soy sauce

1 tablespoon rice wine or dry sherry

1 teaspoon cornstarch, dissolved in
   1 tablespoon water

½ teaspoon sugar

4 teaspoons peanut oil

6 cups green beans, steamed until
   tender-crisp

4 scallions, thinly sliced

1 teaspoon sesame seeds

1. In a small bowl, whisk the soy sauce, wine, dissolved cornstarch, sugar and ¼ cup water until smooth.

2. In a large nonstick skillet or wok, heat 1 tablespoon of the oil until it just begins to smoke, 30–40 seconds. Add the green beans in 2-cup batches; cook, stirring as needed, until lightly browned and the edges are crisp, 1–2 minutes per batch. As it is done, transfer each batch to a plate and keep warm. Wipe out the skillet with a paper towel.

3. Return the skillet to the heat, and heat the remaining 1 teaspoon of the oil. Add the scallions and cook, stirring as needed, until softened, 3–4 minutes. Stir in the green beans and the soy sauce mixture; cook, stirring gently, until the sauce thick-ens and coats the beans. Sprinkle with the sesame seeds; serve at once.

Stir-Fried Spinach

one pot

rush hour

vegetarian

Serving provides:
2 Fruit/Vegetables.

Per serving:
63 Calories,
2 g Total Fat,
0 g Saturated Fat,
0 mg Cholesterol,
327 mg Sodium,
9 g Total Carbohy-
drate, 6 g Dietary
Fiber, 7 g Protein,
224 mg Calcium.

Points per serving: 0.

This quick and savory treatment works well on just about any leafy green; try it with mustard or turnip greens, bok choy or collards, or any other combination.

1 teaspoon peanut oil

½ teaspoon minced peeled gingerroot

1 garlic clove, finely minced

One 10-ounce bag spinach, cleaned and torn into bite-size pieces

1 tablespoon reduced-sodium soy sauce

1 tablespoon rice vinegar

Pinch crushed red pepper flakes

In a large nonstick skillet or wok, heat the oil. Add the ginger and garlic; cook, stir-ring as needed, until just fragrant (do not burn), about 15 seconds. Add the spin-ach, soy sauce, vinegar and pepper flakes; cook, stirring gently, until the spinach is just wilted, about 2 minutes. Serve at once.

Sesame-Walnut Mustard Greens

makes 4 servings

one pot

rush hour

vegetarian

Serving (¾ cup) provides:
1 Fruit/Vegetable,
1 Fat.

Per serving:
84 Calories,
7 g Total Fat,
1 g Saturated Fat,
0 mg Cholesterol,
118 mg Sodium,
4 g Total Carbohy-
drate, 3 g Dietary
Fiber, 4 g Protein,
86 mg Calcium.

Points per serving: 2.

Peppery mustard greens are a perfect match for the rich flavors of sesame and walnut, or substitute other assertive greens, like collards and turnip greens, or broccoli rabe, the slightly bitter Italian broccoli.

1 teaspoon peanut oil

1 garlic clove, minced

3 cups steamed mustard greens

¼ cup walnuts, toasted* and coarsely chopped

2 teaspoons reduced-sodium soy sauce

1 teaspoon Asian sesame oil

1. In a large nonstick skillet or wok, heat the peanut oil. Add the garlic and cook, stirring frequently, about 15 seconds, until just fragrant (do not burn). Add the mustard greens and cook, stirring as needed, until heated through, 1–2 minutes.

2. Sprinkle with the walnuts, soy sauce and sesame oil; toss to coat. Serve at once.

To toast the walnuts, preheat the oven to 350° F. Spread the walnuts in a shallow baking pan; bake, stirring as needed, until golden brown, 8–10 minutes.

Broccoli in Oyster Sauce

makes 4 servings

one pot

rush hour

vegetarian

Serving provides:
1 Fruit/Vegetable,
1 Fat.

Per serving:
70 Calories,
3 g Total Fat,
0 g Saturated Fat,
0 mg Cholesterol,
532 mg Sodium,
10 g Total
Carbohydrate,
3 g Dietary Fiber,
4 g Protein,
52 mg Calcium.

Points per serving: 1.

Once you've mastered this classic recipe, try it on any vegetable. It's well worth having oyster sauce in your refrigerator; it lasts indefinitely and provides an easy sauce for poultry, fish, vegetables or even plain rice.

2 tablespoons oyster sauce*

1 tablespoon reduced-sodium soy sauce

1 tablespoon rice vinegar

2 teaspoons cornstarch

1 teaspoon sugar

1 teaspoon Asian sesame oil

1 teaspoon peanut oil

4 scallions, thinly sliced

½ teaspoon minced peeled gingerroot

1 garlic clove, minced

4 cups broccoli florets and stems, sliced
   into 2" pieces and steamed until
   tender-crisp

1. In a small bowl, whisk the oyster sauce, soy sauce, vinegar, cornstarch, sugar, sesame oil and 2 tablespoons water until smooth.

2. In a large nonstick skillet or wok, heat the peanut oil. Add the scallions, ginger and garlic; cook, stirring as needed, until the scallions are softened, 3–4 minutes. Add the broccoli and cook, tossing lightly, 1 minute. Stir in the oyster sauce mixture; cook, stirring gently, until the sauce thickens and coats the broccoli, about 1 minute. Serve at once.

*See Glossary, page 133.

Pearl Balls and Vegetable Dumpling "Logs" with Peanut Sauce

Stir-Fried Rice Noodles with Chicken, Mushrooms and Leeks

Grilled Garlic Shrimp

Curried Fried Rice

Buddha's Delight

Red-Cooked Pork with Pineapple

Lamb Satays with Peanut Dipping Sauce

Moo Shu Turkey

chapter 5

RED-COOKED AND STEAMED DISHES

Lamb with Leeks

makes 4 servings

If you love the hearty flavors of lamb and leeks, this is the dish for you. Make it on a cool spring Sunday, when you have time to let supper simmer.

8 scallions, cut into 1" lengths

⅓ cup reduced-sodium soy sauce

3 tablespoons rice wine or dry sherry

6 garlic cloves, crushed

1 tablespoon sugar

1 teaspoon light molasses

1 red chile pepper

1 small star anise* clove

2¼ pounds trimmed lamb shanks

4 leeks, cleaned, halved and cut into 1" lengths

1 tablespoon cornstarch, dissolved in 2 tablespoons water

1. In a medium saucepan, bring the scallions, soy sauce, wine, garlic, sugar, molasses, chile pepper, star anise and 3 cups water to a boil. Reduce the heat and simmer, partially covered, about 10 minutes.

2. Add the lamb and simmer, covered, until tender, about 1¼ hours. Add the leeks and cook, covered, until the leeks are tender, about 15 minutes. With a slotted spoon, transfer the lamb and leeks to a plate. Bring the liquid to a boil; stir in the dissolved cornstarch and cook, stirring constantly, until slightly thickened, about 2 minutes. Remove and discard the pepper and anise. When ready to serve, top the lamb and leeks with the sauce.

make ahead

one pot

Serving provides:
1 Fruit/Vegetable,
3 Protein/Milks,
40 Bonus Calories.

Per serving:
327 Calories,
5 g Total Fat,
2 g Saturated Fat,
73 mg Cholesterol,
906 mg Sodium,
40 g Total
Carbohydrate,
3 g Dietary Fiber,
28 g Protein,
152 mg Calcium.

Points per serving: 6.

*See Glossary, page 133.

The Story Behind Red-Cooked

A popular Chinese technique, red-cooking involves braising meat or poultry in a soy sauce–based cooking liquid (usually a mixture of soy sauce, rice wine or sake, sugar, and spices like star anise and cinnamon) to give the food a reddish color and tender flavor. These slow-cooked meats are often served at room temperature or cold.

Red-Cooked Pork with Pineapple

makes 4 servings

Pork and pineapple have a natural affinity, which red-cooking makes the most of.

8 scallions, minced

⅓ cup unsweetened pineapple juice

3 tablespoons hoisin sauce

2 tablespoons minced peeled gingerroot

2 tablespoons reduced-sodium soy sauce

2 tablespoons ketchup

3 garlic cloves, minced

One 1-pound boneless pork butt, trimmed

1 carrot, thinly sliced

1 green bell pepper, seeded and cut into 1" pieces

½ cup drained canned unsweetened pineapple chunks

1. In a medium saucepan, bring the scallions, pineapple juice, hoisin sauce, ginger, soy sauce, ketchup, garlic and ¾ cup water to a boil. Reduce the heat; add the pork and simmer, covered, until the pork is almost tender, about 45 minutes.

2. Add the carrot, pepper and pineapple chunks; cook, covered, until the pork and vegetables are tender, about 15 minutes. Transfer the pork to a cutting board and slice into 12 equal pieces. Serve with the vegetables and sauce.

make ahead

one pot

Serving provides:
1 Fruit/Vegetable,
3 Protein/Milks.

Per serving:
268 Calories,
9 g Total Fat,
3 g Saturated Fat,
72 mg Cholesterol,
712 mg Sodium,
24 g Total Carbohydrate,
2 g Dietary Fiber,
22 g Protein,
58 mg Calcium.

Points per serving: 6.

(See photo insert.)

Pork with Curry and Baby Corn

makes 4 servings

Hoisin sauce, a thick, reddish-brown sauce made of soybean paste, sugar, vinegar, garlic and other flavorings, gives this dish its sweet-and-spicy tang.

3 tablespoons reduced-sodium soy sauce

3 tablespoons hoisin sauce

2 tablespoons rice wine or dry sherry

2 teaspoons sugar

2 garlic cloves, peeled and crushed

¾ teaspoon curry powder

One 1-pound boneless pork shoulder, trimmed

2 cups baby carrots

2 cups drained rinsed canned baby corn ears

4 teaspoons cornstarch, dissolved in 2 tablespoons water

1. In a medium skillet with a tight-fitting lid, bring the soy sauce, hoisin sauce, wine, sugar, garlic, curry and 1¼ cups water to a boil. Reduce the heat; add the pork and simmer, covered, turning the pork several times, until tender and cooked through, about 1 hour. Add the carrots and corn; cook, covered, until the vegetables are tender, about 5 minutes.

2. With a slotted spoon, transfer the pork and vegetables to a platter. Skim off any fat that forms on the surface of the sauce. Bring the liquid to a boil; stir in the dissolved cornstarch and cook, stirring constantly, until the sauce is slightly thickened, about 1 minute.

3. Cut the pork into 4 equal pieces; serve with the vegetables, topped with the sauce.

make ahead

one pot

Serving provides:
1 Bread, 1 Fruit/Vegetable, 3 Protein/Milks.

Per serving:
285 Calories,
8 g Total Fat,
2 g Saturated Fat,
69 mg Cholesterol,
821 mg Sodium,
24 g Total Carbohydrate,
6 g Dietary Fiber,
25 g Protein,
83 mg Calcium.

Points per serving: 5.

Soy-Braised Chicken

makes 8 servings

This incredibly easy, delicious dish is equally good hot, cold or, as the Chinese serve it, at room temperature.

4 scallions, cut into 3" lengths

3 tablespoons reduced-sodium soy sauce

3 tablespoons rice vinegar

2 tablespoons sugar

¼ teaspoon five-spice powder*

One 8" strip orange zest

One 3-pound chicken, cut into 8 equal pieces

2 teaspoons cornstarch, dissolved in 1 tablespoon water

Orange sections, to garnish

1. In a large, heavy saucepan, bring the scallions, soy sauce, vinegar, sugar, five-spice powder, orange zest and ½ cup water to a boil. Add the chicken, turning the pieces to coat, and bring to just below boiling. Reduce the heat and simmer, partially covered, turning the chicken occasionally, until the juices run clear when the chicken is pierced in the thickest part with a fork, 45–50 minutes. With a slotted spoon, transfer the chicken to a serving platter; pour the cooking liquid into a small bowl.

2. Skim off any fat that forms on the surface of the cooking liquid and strain back into the saucepan, discarding the solids. Bring to a boil; stir in the dissolved cornstarch and cook, stirring constantly, until the sauce is slightly thickened, about 1 minute. Drizzle the sauce evenly over the chicken; garnish with orange sections. Remove the skin before eating.

make ahead

one pot

Serving provides:
2 Protein/Milks.

Per serving:
128 Calories,
4 g Total Fat,
1 g Saturated Fat,
50 mg Cholesterol,
274 mg Sodium,
5 g Total Carbohy-
drate, 0 g Dietary
Fiber, 17 g Protein,
13 mg Calcium.

Points per serving: 3.

*See Glossary, page 133.

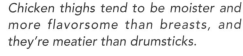

Chicken with Mushrooms, Ginger and Scallions

makes 4 servings

Chicken thighs tend to be moister and more flavorsome than breasts, and they're meatier than drumsticks.

⅓ cup reduced-sodium soy sauce

¼ cup minced peeled gingerroot

3 tablespoons sugar

Three 3 x ½" strips dried orange rind*

1½ pounds chicken thighs (about 4), skinned

3 cups trimmed small white mushrooms

2 cups sliced shiitake mushrooms

1 green bell pepper, seeded and thinly sliced

16 scallions, sliced

1 tablespoon cornstarch, dissolved in 2 tablespoons water

1. In a medium saucepan, bring the soy sauce, ginger, sugar, orange rind and 2½ cups water to a boil. Reduce the heat and simmer, partially covered, until the flavors are blended, about 30 minutes.

2. Add the chicken, white mushrooms, shiitake mushrooms and pepper; cook, uncovered, until the juices run clear when the chicken is pierced in the thickest part with a fork, about 25 minutes. Cover and let stand about 15 minutes.

3. With a slotted spoon, transfer the chicken and vegetables to 4 plates; discard the orange rind. Bring the liquid to a boil; stir in the dissolved cornstarch and cook, stirring constantly, until the sauce is slightly thickened, about 1 minute. Spoon the sauce evenly over the chicken and vegetables.

make ahead

one pot

Serving provides:
2 Fruit/Vegetables,
3 Protein/Milks.

Per serving:
225 Calories,
5 g Total Fat,
1 g Saturated Fat,
88 mg Cholesterol,
893 mg Sodium,
22 g Total
Carbohydrate,
2 g Dietary Fiber,
25 g Protein,
44 mg Calcium.

Points per serving: 5.

*See Glossary, page 133.

Red-Cooked Chicken, Vegetables and Tofu

makes 4 servings

Snow peas have a fairly tough string down the inside of the pod. The easiest way to trim it is to snap the stem gently and pull toward the opposite end of the pod.

5 dried Chinese black mushrooms caps*
  (about ½ ounce)

2 cups low-sodium chicken broth

3 tablespoons reduced-sodium soy
  sauce

2 tablespoons rice wine or dry sherry

2 teaspoons Asian sesame oil

1 tablespoon firmly packed light brown
  sugar

Two 3 x ½" strips orange zest*

One 2" cinnamon stick

1½ pounds chicken thighs (about 4),
  skinned

2 carrots, thinly sliced

1 cup trimmed snow peas

¼ pound firm reduced-fat tofu, cut into
  1" chunks

1 tablespoon cornstarch, dissolved in
  2 tablespoons water

8 scallions, minced

1. In a small saucepan, bring 1 cup water to a boil. Add the mushrooms; cover and remove from heat. Let stand until softened, about 20 minutes. Drain, reserving ½ cup of the soaking liquid. Strain the liquid through a cheesecloth-lined strainer.

2. In a medium saucepan, bring the broth, soaking liquid, soy sauce, wine, oil, brown sugar, orange zest and cinnamon to a boil. Reduce the heat and simmer, covered, until the flavors are blended, about 20 minutes. Add the chicken and simmer, covered, until the juices run clear when the chicken is pierced in the thickest part with a fork, about 40 minutes. Add the carrots and cook about 5 minutes longer; add the snow peas, the mushrooms and tofu; cook 1 minute longer.

3. With a slotted spoon, transfer the chicken, tofu and vegetables to 4 plates. Bring the liquid to a boil, stir in the dissolved cornstarch and cook, stirring constantly, until the sauce is slightly thickened, about 1 minute. Add the scallions. Spoon the sauce evenly over the chicken mixture.

See Glossary, page 133.

make ahead

Serving provides:
1 Fruit/Vegetable,
3 Protein/Milks,
1 Fat.

Per serving:
290 Calories,
10 g Total Fat,
2 g Saturated Fat,
88 mg Cholesterol,
628 mg Sodium,
20 g Total
Carbohydrate,
4 g Dietary Fiber,
30 g Protein,
129 mg Calcium.

Points per serving: 6.

Red-Cooked Chicken with Cabbage

makes 4 servings

Even if you steer clear of napa cabbage because you're not fond of green cabbage, try it in this dish. Napa's lighter flavor and more delicate texture shine in this hearty meal.

make ahead

one pot

Serving provides:
1 Bread, 1 Fruit/
Vegetable, 3 Protein/
Milks, 1 Fat.

Per serving:
293 Calories,
7 g Total Fat,
2 g Saturated Fat,
94 mg Cholesterol,
665 mg Sodium,
27 g Total
Carbohydrate,
2 g Dietary Fiber,
28 g Protein,
96 mg Calcium.

Points per serving: 6.

3 tablespoons reduced-sodium soy sauce

2 tablespoons firmly packed light brown sugar

2 tablespoons rice wine or dry sherry

8 garlic cloves, peeled and crushed

2 teaspoons Asian sesame oil

One 2" piece peeled gingerroot, thinly sliced

1½ pounds whole chicken legs (about 3), split, skinned and boned

¼ cup chopped smoked ham

4 cups napa or Savoy cabbage, cut into 1" chunks

2 small all-purpose potatoes, peeled and cut into ½" chunks

1 tablespoon cornstarch, dissolved in 2 tablespoons water

1. In a large saucepan, bring the soy sauce, brown sugar, wine, garlic, oil, ginger and 3 cups of water to a boil. Reduce the heat and simmer, uncovered, about 10 minutes. Add the chicken and ham; return to a boil. Reduce the heat and simmer, covered, until the chicken is almost cooked through, about 25 minutes. Add the cabbage and potatoes; cook, covered, until the chicken is cooked through and the cabbage is tender, about 10 minutes.

2. With a slotted spoon, transfer the chicken, cabbage and potatoes to 4 plates. Bring the liquid to a boil, stir in the dissolved cornstarch and cook, stirring constantly, until the sauce is slightly thickened, about 1 minute. Spoon the sauce evenly over the chicken and vegetables.

Chinese-Glazed Hens

makes 4 servings

Although quail are more traditional, game hens are much easier to find, and they're a nice change from chicken.

Two 1-pound Cornish game hens, halved

3 tablespoons reduced-sodium
  soy sauce

1 tablespoon + 2 teaspoons honey

1 teaspoon five-spice powder*

one pot

Serving provides:
3 Protein/Milks.

Per serving:
198 Calories,
6 g Total Fat,
2 g Saturated Fat,
76 mg Cholesterol,
524 mg Sodium,
9 g Total Carbohy-
drate, 0 g Dietary
Fiber, 25 g Protein,
16 mg Calcium.

Points per serving: 4.

1. Preheat the oven to 400° F. Line a roasting pan with foil and place a rack in the pan. Place the hens, skin-side down, on the rack.

2. In a small bowl, combine the soy sauce, honey and five-spice powder. Brush the inside of the hens evenly with one-fourth of the soy sauce mixture. Roast about 10 minutes; then turn the hens and brush the skins with another one-fourth of the mixture. Roast, brushing the hens every 5 minutes, using all of the remaining soy sauce mixture, until the juices run clear when the hens are pierced in the thickest part with a fork, 15–20 minutes. Serve warm or at room temperature; remove the skin before eating.

See Glossary, page 133.

Pearl Balls

makes 4 servings

These pretty little gems get their name from the grains of rice they're rolled in, which swell up into pearl-like grains as they steam. They're great finger food for a cocktail party. Be sure to use only sticky rice (sometimes called "sweet" or "glutinous" rice); available at Asian markets, it has the proper stickiness that enables it to cling to the meatballs.

⅔ cup sticky rice*

2 dried Chinese black mushroom caps*

10 ounces lean ground pork

¾ cup water chestnuts, coarsely chopped

½ carrot, shredded

2 scallions, thinly sliced

1 tablespoon soy sauce

2 teaspoons cornstarch

1 teaspoon Asian sesame oil

One ½" piece peeled gingerroot, minced

1. Place the rice in a strainer. Rinse with cold running water, stirring with your fingers until the water is clear. Drain the rice and transfer to a bowl. Cover with 2" of cold water; let soak 1 hour. Drain the rice and spread on a baking sheet.

2. In a small saucepan, bring ¾ cup water to a boil; add the mushrooms. Cover and remove from heat. Let stand until softened, about 20 minutes. Drain, discarding the liquid, and finely chop the mushrooms.

3. In a large bowl, lightly combine the pork, water chestnuts, carrot, the mushrooms, scallions, soy sauce, cornstarch, oil and ginger. Shape the mixture into 24 equal meatballs, about 1" each.

4. Roll each meatball in the rice to cover it completely; with your fingers, gently press the rice grains into each meatball.

5. In a large saucepan, bring 2" of water to a boil. Line a steamer rack with cheesecloth and moisten it with water. Arrange 12 of the meatballs on the steamer rack about 1" apart; place in the saucepan and cover with a tight-fitting lid. Steam, adding more water if necessary, until the meatballs are cooked through and the rice grains are translucent, 20–25 minutes. Transfer to a serving plate and keep warm. Replenish the water in the steamer and repeat with the remaining meatballs. (If your saucepan is large enough, steam all the meatballs at the same time.)

*See Glossary, page 133.

make ahead

Serving provides:
1 Bread, 2 Protein/
Milks, 50 Bonus
Calories.

Per serving:
267 Calories,
7 g Total Fat,
2 g Saturated Fat,
47 mg Cholesterol,
322 mg Sodium,
33 g Total
Carbohydrate,
2 g Dietary Fiber,
17 g Protein,
18 mg Calcium.

Points per serving: 6.

(See photo insert.)

Cooking Utensils

The right gadgets can make cooking Chinese cuisine easier. Consider investing in the following:

- **Bamboo Steamer:** This steamer consists of a two-tier bamboo basket with an open weave, a rimmed bottom and a tightly woven bamboo lid. The steamer works on the same principle as a double boiler. After the food is placed in the steamer basket, the basket is suspended over a pot of boiling water so the rising steam cooks the food.

- **Handled Strainer:** A wire-mesh basket with a bamboo handle, the strainer is used to remove cooked food from hot oil or water. The food is often allowed to "rest" or drain in the strainer (placed over a bowl or pan). Although a slotted spoon used in conjunction with a bowl makes an acceptable substitution, the strainer tends to hold more food.

- **Shovel:** A spatula with slanted sides designed to conform to the shape of a wok, a shovel is used for stir-frying and mixing ingredients.

- **Cleaver:** This is an all-purpose cutting instrument for the Asian chef: The sharp edge cuts, the sides of the blade flatten and the blunt edge tenderizes food. The cleaver is sold in a variety of sizes and weights—the smallest and lightest cleaver is used for cutting vegetables, the medium-weight one is used for such tasks as cutting meats, and the heaviest grade is reserved for tough jobs like cutting through bones.

Steamed Cod Fillets with Black-Bean Sauce

makes 4 servings

Cod steams beautifully, and its mild flavor really wakes up with this spicy sauce. Other firm, white-fleshed fish like snapper or haddock make fine substitutes.

2 tablespoons rice wine or dry sherry

1 teaspoon soy sauce

One 1" piece peeled gingerroot, minced

4 small (5-ounce) pieces cod fillets,
    1" thick

2 teaspoons peanut oil

2 scallions, minced

1 tablespoon fermented black beans,*
    rinsed, drained and finely chopped

1 garlic clove, minced

½ teaspoon sugar

¼ teaspoon hot chili paste*

2 teaspoons cornstarch, dissolved in
    1 tablespoon water

1 tablespoon minced cilantro (optional)

1. To prepare the marinade, in a gallon-size sealable plastic bag, combine 1 tablespoon of the wine, the soy sauce and ginger; add the cod. Seal the bag, squeezing out the air; turn to coat the cod. Refrigerate about 30 minutes, turning the bag occasionally. Drain the cod, reserving the marinade; place the fillets in a pie plate or pan large enough to fit a steamer rack.

2. To prepare the sauce, place a medium nonstick skillet or wok, heat the oil. Add the scallions, black beans and garlic; cook, stirring as needed, until the scallions begin to soften, about 1 minute. Stir in the marinade, the remaining 1 tablespoon of the wine, the sugar and chili paste; bring to a boil and cook, stirring gently, about 1 minute. Spread the sauce evenly over the fish; set the skillet aside.

3. In a large saucepan, bring 2" of water to a boil. Set the pie plate on the steamer rack; place in the saucepan and cover with a tight-fitting lid. Steam until the fish flakes easily when tested with a fork, about 10 minutes. With a slotted spatula, carefully transfer the fish to a serving platter.

4. Carefully pour the pan juices into the skillet; bring to a boil and stir in the dissolved cornstarch. Cook, stirring constantly, until the sauce is thickened, about 1 minute. Pour the sauce evenly over the fish and sprinkle with the cilantro (if using); serve at once.

spicy

Serving provides:
2 Protein/Milks,
1 Fat.

Per serving:
160 Calories,
3 g Total Fat,
1 g Saturated Fat,
61 mg Cholesterol,
281 mg Sodium,
3 g Total Carbohydrate, 0 g Dietary Fiber, 26 g Protein,
31 mg Calcium.

Points per serving: 3.

*See Glossary, page 133.

Steamed Clams with Spicy Dipping Sauce

makes 4 servings

Buy only the freshest live clams for this simple dish, so their clear, briny flavor can shine through. Make sure the shells are tightly closed; if a shell is slightly open, tap it lightly. If it doesn't snap shut immediately, the clam is dead and should be discarded.

2 tablespoons cornmeal

24 steamers or littleneck clams, scrubbed

2 tablespoons white vinegar

1 tablespoon reduced-sodium soy sauce

1 teaspoon cornstarch

1 teaspoon sugar

1 teaspoon ketchup

½ teaspoon Asian sesame oil

½ garlic clove, minced

1 scallion, minced

1 tablespoon minced cilantro

spicy

Serving provides:
1 Protein/Milk.

Per serving:
59 Calories,
1 g Total Fat,
0 g Saturated Fat,
19 mg Cholesterol,
197 mg Sodium,
4 g Total Carbohy-
drate, 0 g Dietary
Fiber, 8 g Protein,
29 mg Calcium.

Points per serving: 1.

1. In a large saucepan, stir the cornmeal into 8 cups cold water; add the clams and refrigerate 1 hour. Drain and rinse the clams.

2. In the saucepan, bring 1" of water to a boil. Add the clams and cook, shaking the pan occasionally, until the clams begin to open, 7–10 minutes. Remove each clam as it opens and transfer to a serving platter; keep warm. Discard any clams that have not opened after 10 minutes. Pour the liquid remaining in the saucepan into a measuring cup; add water, if necessary, to make ½ cup.

3. To prepare the sauce, in a small saucepan, whisk the clam liquid, vinegar, soy sauce, cornstarch, sugar, ketchup, oil and garlic until smooth. Bring to a boil; reduce the heat and cook until slightly thickened, 1–2 minutes. Transfer to a small serving bowl. To serve, sprinkle the clams evenly with the scallion and cilantro. Serve with the dipping sauce on the side.

Steamed Eggplant

makes 4 servings

Steaming eggplant makes it unusually sweet and tender, yet doesn't add a bit of fat. Use this technique whenever sautéed eggplant is called for in a recipe; you'll save oodles of calories and fat grams. If you find the small, lavender-color Chinese eggplant in your supermarket or Asian grocery store, use them instead—they'll have a slightly firmer texture when cooked. You can also puree this in a food processor to make a wonderful dip for cut-up vegetables and bread.

1 medium (1¼-pound) eggplant, peeled and cut into 1½" cubes

2 tablespoons low-sodium vegetable broth

1 scallion, minced

1 tablespoon reduced-sodium soy sauce

1 tablespoon rice wine or dry sherry

1 tablespoon rice vinegar

1 teaspoon sugar

1 teaspoon Dijon mustard

1 garlic clove, minced

Pinch crushed red pepper flakes

2 teaspoons minced cilantro (optional)

1. In a large saucepan, bring 2" of water to a boil. Arrange the eggplant cubes in an even layer on a steamer rack; place in the saucepan and cover with a tight-fitting lid. Steam until just tender when pierced with a fork but not completely translucent, 4–5 minutes. Transfer to a colander; let stand in the sink about 5 minutes to drain, then place in a medium serving bowl.

2. In a small bowl, whisk the broth, scallion, soy sauce, wine, vinegar, sugar, mustard, garlic and pepper flakes until smooth. Pour over the eggplant and toss lightly to coat. Let stand until the flavors are blended, about 30 minutes. Sprinkle with the cilantro (if using); serve at once.

one pot

vegetarian

Serving provides:
1 Fruit/Vegetable.

Per serving:
39 Calories,
0 g Total Fat,
0 g Saturated Fat,
0 mg Cholesterol,
188 mg Sodium,
8 g Total Carbohy-
drate, 1 g Dietary
Fiber, 1 g Protein,
37 mg Calcium.

Points per serving: 1.

chapter 6

GRILLED DISHES

Beef-Scallion Burgers

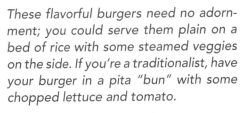

one pot

rush hour

Serving provides:
3 Protein/Milks.

Per serving:
203 Calories,
11 g Total Fat,
4 g Saturated Fat,
66 mg Cholesterol,
303 mg Sodium,
4 g Total Carbohy-
drate, 0 g Dietary
Fiber, 22 g Protein,
8 mg Calcium.

Points per serving: 5.

*These flavorful burgers need no adorn-
ment; you could serve them plain on a
bed of rice with some steamed veggies
on the side. If you're a traditionalist, have
your burger in a pita "bun" with some
chopped lettuce and tomato.*

1 pound lean ground beef (10% or
    less fat)

4 scallions, thinly sliced

¼ cup water chestnuts, finely chopped

2 teaspoons soy sauce

2 teaspoons hoisin sauce

1 garlic clove, minced

½ teaspoon minced peeled gingerroot

1. Spray the broiler or grill rack with nonstick cooking spray; set aside. Preheat the
broiler or grill.

2. In a medium bowl, lightly combine the
beef, scallions, water chestnuts, soy sauce,
hoisin sauce, garlic and ginger. Refrigerate, covered, until the flavors are blended,
about 10 minutes. Shape into 4 equal
burgers.

3. Grill the burgers on the prepared rack,
5" from the heat, turning once, 6 minutes (rare), 8 minutes (medium) or 10
minutes (well-done); serve at once.

Mongolian Barbecued Beef

makes 6 servings

Mongolian Barbecue is one of the most famous dishes to come out of this remote part of northern China. It's traditionally served hot off the grill and stuffed into warm, sesame seed–studded flatbread; you can use warm sesame pita bread with good results.

¼ cup boiling water

1 tablespoon + 1 teaspoon minced peeled gingerroot

2 tablespoons reduced-sodium soy sauce

1 tablespoon hoisin sauce

1 tablespoon rice wine or dry sherry

1½ teaspoons Asian sesame oil

1 teaspoon firmly packed dark brown sugar

1 garlic clove, minced

1 pound trimmed beef sirloin or tenderloin, cut into thin 2" squares

4 cups bean sprouts

12 scallions, thinly sliced

6 small sesame pitas, warmed

Serving provides:
1 Bread, 1 Fruit/Vegetable, 2 Protein/Milks.

Per serving:
245 Calories,
6 g Total Fat,
2 g Saturated Fat,
50 mg Cholesterol,
449 mg Sodium,
24 g Total Carbohydrate,
2 g Dietary Fiber,
23 g Protein,
58 mg Calcium.

Points per serving: 5.

1. In a small heatproof bowl, combine the boiling water and 1 tablespoon of the ginger; cover and let steep about 10 minutes. Strain, discarding the solids, and set the ginger water aside.

2. To prepare the marinade, in a quart-size sealable plastic bag, combine the soy sauce, hoisin sauce, wine, oil, brown sugar, the remaining 1 teaspoon of the ginger and the garlic; add the beef. Seal the bag, squeezing out the air; turn to coat the beef. Refrigerate 1 hour, turning the bag occasionally.

3. Line the grill rack with several layers of foil; pierce in several places with a toothpick. Spray with nonstick cooking spray; set aside. Preheat the grill.

4. Drain the beef, discarding the marinade. Grill one-fourth of the beef, 5" from the coals, about 15 seconds. Sprinkle with one-fourth each of the bean sprouts and scallions. Toss the mixture gently with chopsticks. Continue tossing until the beef is nearly cooked through, about 1 minute, and transfer to a serving platter. Repeat with the remaining beef, bean sprouts and scallions. Return the entire mixture to the grill and sprinkle with the ginger water; toss 1 minute to combine. Serve, with the pitas on the side.

Sesame-Garlic Flank Steak

makes 6 servings

Made from ground sesame seeds, tahini is popular in Middle Eastern cooking. It's used in hummus and baba ghanoush, but it also adds delicious flavor to this easy steak.

2 tablespoons reduced-sodium
    soy sauce

2 tablespoons tahini (sesame paste)

1 tablespoon minced peeled gingerroot

2 garlic cloves, minced

1¼ pounds flank steak, trimmed and cut
    into 12 equal slices

make ahead

Serving provides:
3 Protein/Milks.

Per serving:
179 Calories,
9 g Total Fat,
4 g Saturated Fat,
52 mg Cholesterol,
168 mg Sodium,
1 g Total Carbohy-
drate, 0 g Dietary
Fiber, 22 g Protein,
18 mg Calcium.

Points per serving: 4.

1. To prepare the marinade, in a gallon-size sealable plastic bag, combine the soy sauce, tahini, ginger and garlic; add the steak. Seal the bag, squeezing out the air; turn to coat the steak. Refrigerate at least 1 hour, turning the bag occasionally.

2. Spray the grill rack with nonstick cooking spray; set aside. Prepare the grill.

3. If using wooden skewers, soak six 10–12" skewers in enough water to cover for about 15 minutes (to prevent burning).

4. Drain the steak, discarding the marinade. Thread 2 slices of steak onto each skewer. Grill the steak, 5" from the heat, turning as needed, until done to taste, 6–7 minutes; serve at once.

Spicy Lamb Kebabs

makes 4 servings

If you like shish kebab, you'll love it with this Chinese twist. Serve it with plenty of rice or warm flatbreads.

1 teaspoon Szechuan peppercorns*

1 tablespoon reduced-sodium soy sauce

1 tablespoon rice wine or dry sherry

1 teaspoon Asian sesame oil

½ teaspoon five-spice powder*

One ½" piece peeled gingerroot, minced

1 garlic clove, minced

10 ounces boneless lamb shoulder, trimmed and cut into 1" cubes

16 cherry tomatoes

1 green bell pepper, seeded and cut into 1" pieces

1. Place a small nonstick skillet over medium-high heat. Toast the peppercorns, shaking the pan, until they begin to smoke, about 1 minute. Crush in a mortar and pestle or a spice grinder. Sift through a fine sieve and discard the shells, reserving the powder.

2. To prepare the marinade, in a gallon-size sealable plastic bag, combine the soy sauce, wine, oil, peppercorn powder, five-spice powder, ginger and garlic; add the lamb. Seal the bag, squeezing out the air; turn to coat the lamb. Refrigerate 1 hour, turning the bag occasionally.

3. Spray the broiler or grill rack with non-stick cooking spray; set aside. Preheat the broiler or grill.

4. If using wooden skewers, soak eight 10–12" skewers in enough water to cover for about 15 minutes (to prevent burning).

5. Drain the marinade into a small sauce-pan and bring to a rolling boil; boil for 1 minute, stirring constantly. Remove from the heat and set aside.

6. Thread the lamb, tomatoes and pepper evenly onto the skewers in an alternating pattern. Brush with the marinade and grill on the prepared rack, 5" from the heat, turning occasionally and brushing with the marinade, until the meat is browned, 8–10 minutes; serve at once.

spicy

Serving provides:
1 Fruit/Vegetable,
2 Protein/Milks.

Per serving:
155 Calories,
6 g Total Fat,
2 g Saturated Fat,
52 mg Cholesterol,
202 mg Sodium,
6 g Total Carbohy-
drate, 1 g Dietary
Fiber, 17 g Protein,
21 mg Calcium.

Points per serving: 3.

*See Glossary, page 133.

Tea Time

When you visit a Chinese home, it isn't long before you're offered a cup of tea. Indeed, tea drinking first began in China, and it's still an important ritual.

There are more than 250 kinds of Chinese teas, but basically they all fall into three categories: black tea, made from fermented tea leaves, with a strong, assertive flavor; green tea, made from dried, unfermented leaves, producing a delicate, grassy taste; and oolong tea, whose leaves are fermented only a short time, resulting in a green-brown color and distinctive, slightly grassy flavor.

Getting into the tea-drinking habit may give you also a health boost in the bargain. Compounds found in tea, called polyphenols, may have important health benefits. Polyphenols appear to act like antioxidants, helping to prevent the cell-damaging processes in cancers and heart disease, and they may help prevent cancer-causing chemicals from becoming activated. Polyphenols are most abundant in green tea, but black and oolong teas, as well as decaffeinated teas, also contain healthy amounts.

Lamb Satays with Peanut Dipping Sauce

makes 4 servings

Although satays originated in Indonesia, we've given them Chinese flair and lightened the traditional salty–sweet peanut sauce by adding pureed chickpeas. The dramatic dish serves four as an entrée, eight as a satisfying appetizer.

Satays:

1 tablespoon reduced-sodium soy sauce

1 tablespoon fresh lime juice

2 teaspoons peanut oil

One ½" piece peeled gingerroot, minced

1 garlic clove, minced

¼ teaspoon ground cumin

¼ teaspoon hot chili paste*

¾ pound boneless lamb shoulder, trimmed and cut into 16 long, thin strips

Dipping Sauce:

¼ cup drained rinsed canned chickpeas

2 tablespoons fresh lime juice

2 tablespoons natural peanut butter

1 tablespoon reduced-sodium soy sauce

2 teaspoons firmly packed dark brown sugar

2 garlic cloves, minced

¼ teaspoon hot chili paste*

spicy

Serving provides:
3 Protein/Milks,
1 Fat.

Per serving:
240 Calories,
12 g Total Fat,
3 g Saturated Fat,
59 mg Cholesterol,
403 mg Sodium,
10 g Total
Carbohydrate,
1 g Dietary Fiber,
22 g Protein,
26 mg Calcium.

Points per serving: 6.

(See photo insert.)

1. To prepare the marinade, in a gallon-size sealable plastic bag, combine the soy sauce, lime juice, oil, ginger, garlic, cumin and chili paste; add the lamb. Seal the bag, squeezing out the air; turn to coat the lamb. Refrigerate 1 hour, turning the bag occasionally.

2. Spray the broiler or grill rack with non-stick cooking spray; set aside. Preheat the broiler or grill.

3. If using wooden skewers, soak sixteen 10–12" skewers in enough water to cover for about 15 minutes (to prevent burning).

4. To prepare the peanut sauce, in a blender or mini food processor, puree the chickpeas, lime juice, peanut butter, soy sauce and brown sugar until smooth.

5. Drain the marinade into a small saucepan and bring to a rolling boil; boil for 1 minute, stirring constantly. Remove from the heat.

6. Thread one lamb strip onto each skewer, piercing the meat in several places and spreading out to lie as flat as possible. Grill the lamb, 5" from the heat, turning once and brushing with the marinade, until browned outside but still juicy inside, 2–3 minutes; serve at once, with the peanut sauce on the side.

---

*See Glossary, page 133.

Barbecued Pork Loin

makes 16 servings

Most pork loin is sold boned, rolled and tied for roasting; for grilling, it's better to have the loin as flat as possible so it cooks evenly and quickly. This classic Cantonese recipe makes enough to feed a large party, with plenty of leftovers for freezing or slicing into sandwiches and salads (or, as the Chinese do, dicing and stuffing into dumplings and steamed buns).

One 2½-pound boneless lean pork loin

1 tablespoon hoisin sauce

1 teaspoon reduced-sodium soy sauce

1 teaspoon rice vinegar

One 1" piece peeled gingerroot, minced

1 garlic clove, minced

1. Place the pork between 2 sheets of wax paper. Pound the pork lightly with a meat mallet to an even thickness (about 2½").

2. To prepare the marinade, in a gallon-size sealable plastic bag, combine the hoisin sauce, soy sauce, vinegar, ginger and garlic; add the pork. Seal the bag, squeezing out the air; turn to coat the pork. Refrigerate at least 2 hours or overnight, turning the bag occasionally.

3. Spray the broiler or grill rack with non-stick cooking spray; set aside. Preheat the broiler or grill.

4. Drain the pork, discarding the marinade. Grill the pork, 5" from the heat, turning occasionally, until almost cooked through, 18–25 minutes. Transfer to a platter and cover with foil; let stand about 10 minutes. Slice thinly and serve at once, or reserve some for later use.

make ahead

one pot

Serving provides:
2 Protein/Milks.

Per serving:
122 Calories,
6 g Total Fat,
2 g Saturated Fat,
45 mg Cholesterol,
69 mg Sodium,
1 g Total Carbohydrate, 0 g Dietary
Fiber, 16 g Protein,
10 mg Calcium.

Points per serving: 3.

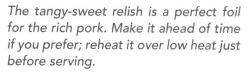

Butterflied Pork with Ginger-Plum Relish

makes 4 servings

The tangy-sweet relish is a perfect foil for the rich pork. Make it ahead of time if you prefer; reheat it over low heat just before serving.

make ahead

one pot

Serving provides:
1 Fruit/Vegetable,
3 Protein/Milks,
1 Fat.

Per serving:
245 Calories,
11 g Total Fat,
3 g Saturated Fat,
67 mg Cholesterol,
55 mg Sodium,
11 g Total
Carbohydrate,
1 g Dietary Fiber,
25 g Protein,
20 mg Calcium.

Points per serving: 6.

2 teaspoons olive oil

1 garlic clove, peeled and crushed

1 teaspoon grated lemon zest

2 teaspoons grated peeled gingerroot

1 teaspoon dry mustard

One 1-pound boneless lean pork loin, trimmed and butterflied

4 teaspoons cider vinegar

1 tablespoon sugar

4 plums, pitted and diced

1. Place the grill rack 5" from the heat; preheat the grill.

2. With a mortar and pestle or in a mini food processor, blend the oil, garlic, lemon zest, 1 teaspoon of the ginger and ½ teaspoon of the mustard to a paste. Rub evenly onto both sides of the pork.

3. Grill the pork, turning once, until cooked through but still juicy, about 20 minutes. Transfer to a carving board; let stand about 5 minutes.

4. Meanwhile, to prepare the relish, in a small nonreactive saucepan, combine the vinegar, sugar, the remaining 1 teaspoon of the ginger and the remaining ½ teaspoon of the mustard; cook, stirring constantly, about 1 minute. Remove from the heat and stir in the plums.

5. Slice the pork and serve, topped with the relish.

Black-Bean Grilled Chicken

makes 6 servings

One problem with grilling a whole chicken is that the outside burns before the inside is done. Parcooking it first can help, or try this even simpler method of splitting the bird in half. You'll have juicy, perfectly cooked chicken in about a half hour. With its flavorful marinade, it's sure to be a crowd pleaser.

One 3½-pound chicken

2 tablespoons reduced-sodium soy
    sauce

2 tablespoons rice wine or dry sherry

1 tablespoon fermented black beans,*
    rinsed, drained and finely chopped

One 1" piece peeled gingerroot, minced

Serving provides:
3 Protein/Milks.

Per serving:
168 Calories,
6 g Total Fat,
2 g Saturated Fat,
76 mg Cholesterol,
210 mg Sodium,
0 g Total Carbohy-
drate, 0 g Dietary
Fiber, 25 g Protein,
15 mg Calcium.

Points per serving: 4.

1. With poultry shears, cut the chicken along the breastbone, then along the backbone, into two halves. Remove the backbone and the end of the breastbone so that the halves lie flat.

2. To prepare the marinade, in a gallon-size sealable plastic bag, combine the soy sauce, wine, black beans and ginger; add the chicken. Seal the bag, squeezing out the air; turn to coat the chicken. Refrigerate about 30 minutes, turning the bag occasionally.

3. Spray the broiler or grill rack with non-stick cooking spray; set aside. Preheat the broiler or grill.

4. Drain the marinade into a small saucepan and bring to a rolling boil; boil for 1 minute, stirring constantly. Remove from the heat.

5. Grill the chicken, 5" from the heat, turning occasionally and brushing with the marinade, until the juices run clear when the chicken is pierced in the thickest part with a fork, 25–30 minutes. Transfer to a serving platter, cover loosely with foil and let stand about 10 minutes. Cut the chicken into 6 equal pieces. Remove the skin before eating.

*See Glossary, page 133.

Lemon-Ginger Grilled Chicken

makes 4 servings

Inspired by the restaurant favorite Lemon Chicken, this heavenly, slightly tart dish can be served hot or cold.

Grated zest of 1 lemon

⅓ cup fresh lemon juice

2 teaspoons minced peeled gingerroot

2 teaspoons firmly packed dark brown sugar

1 teaspoon peanut oil

2 dried Szechuan chile peppers,* seeds removed and discarded

1½ pounds chicken thighs (about 4)

1. To prepare the marinade, in a gallon-size sealable plastic bag, combine the lemon zest, lemon juice, ginger, brown sugar, oil and peppers; add the chicken.

Seal the bag, squeezing out the air; turn to coat the chicken. Refrigerate 1 hour, turning the bag occasionally.

2. Spray the broiler or grill rack with non-stick cooking spray; set aside. Preheat the broiler or grill.

3. Drain the marinade into a small saucepan and bring to a rolling boil for 1 minute, stirring constantly. Remove from the heat.

4. Grill the chicken, 5" from the heat, turning occasionally and brushing with the marinade, until the juices run clear when the chicken is pierced in the thickest part with a fork, 10–12 minutes. Serve, or let cool to room temperature, cover and refrigerate up to 2 days. Remove the skin before eating.

*See Glossary, page 133.

make ahead

Serving provides:
3 Protein/Milks.

Per serving:
192 Calories,
10 g Total Fat,
3 g Saturated Fat,
81 mg Cholesterol,
76 mg Sodium,
2 g Total Carbohydrate, 0 g Dietary Fiber, 22 g Protein,
13 mg Calcium.

Points per serving: 5.

Sesame-Soy Hens

makes 2 servings

This recipe combines the flavors of red-cooking with the speed of grilling.

2 tablespoons cider vinegar

2 tablespoons reduced-sodium soy sauce

1 teaspoon Asian sesame oil

1 teaspoon Dijon mustard

1 teaspoon honey

½ teaspoon minced peeled gingerroot

One 1-pound Cornish game hen, halved

make ahead

one pot

Serving provides:
3 Protein/Milks,
1 Fat.

Per serving:
207 Calories,
9 g Total Fat,
2 g Saturated Fat,
76 mg Cholesterol,
734 mg Sodium,
5 g Total Carbohy-
drate, 0 g Dietary
Fiber, 26 g Protein,
17 mg Calcium.

Points per serving: 5.

1. To prepare the marinade, in a gallon-size sealable plastic bag, combine the vinegar, soy sauce, oil, mustard, honey and ginger; add the hen. Seal the bag, squeezing out the air; turn to coat the hen. Refrigerate at least 1 hour or overnight, turning the bag occasionally.

2. Place the grill rack 5" from the heat; preheat the grill.

3. Drain the marinade into a small sauce-pan and bring to a rolling boil for 1 minute, stirring constantly. Remove from the heat.

4. Grill the hen, turning occasionally and basting with the marinade, until the juices run clear when the hen is pierced in the thickest part with a fork, 20–25 minutes. Remove the skin before eating.

Grilled Salmon with Ginger and Szechuan Peppercorns

makes 4 servings

In this simple preparation, the pungency of ginger and pepper cut through the richness of the salmon beautifully. Serve it with crisp, sweet vegetables like snow peas or carrots and some brown rice.

1 teaspoon Szechuan peppercorns*

1 tablespoon reduced-sodium soy sauce

1 tablespoon rice vinegar

1 teaspoon peanut oil

One 1" piece peeled gingerroot, minced

One 1-pound salmon fillet

Lime wedges (optional)

spicy

Serving provides:
3 Protein/Milks.

Per serving:
166 Calories,
8 g Total Fat,
1 g Saturated Fat,
58 mg Cholesterol,
197 mg Sodium,
1 g Total Carbohy-
drate, 0 g Dietary
Fiber, 21 g Protein,
16 mg Calcium.

Points per serving: 4.

1. In a small nonstick skillet, toast the peppercorns, shaking the pan, until they begin to smoke, about 1 minute. Crush in a mortar and pestle or a spice grinder. Sift through a fine sieve and discard the shells, reserving the powder.

2. To prepare the marinade, in a gallon-size sealable plastic bag, combine the soy sauce, vinegar, peppercorn powder, oil and ginger; add the salmon. Seal the bag, squeezing out the air; turn to coat the salmon. Refrigerate 1 hour, turning the bag occasionally.

3. Spray the broiler or grill rack with non-stick cooking spray; set aside. Preheat the broiler or grill.

4. Drain the marinade into a small saucepan and bring to a rolling boil for 1 minute, stirring constantly. Remove from the heat.

5. Grill the salmon, 5" from the heat, turning once and brushing with the marinade, until browned on the outside but still slightly pink in the center, 7–10 minutes, depending on its thickness. Garnish with lime wedges (if using) and serve at once.

See Glossary, page 133.

Pacific Rim Halibut

makes 6 servings

Halibut are the largest of the flat fish; they have finely textured and extremely lean meat. Because they are so lean, though, take care not to overcook them.

¼ cup honey

2 tablespoons reduced-sodium soy sauce

2 tablespoons fresh lemon juice

1 tablespoon Asian sesame oil

2 garlic cloves, minced

1 teaspoon ground ginger

½ teaspoon dry mustard

½ teaspoon crushed red pepper flakes

¼ teaspoon freshly ground black pepper

Six ½-pound halibut steaks

spicy

Serving provides:
3 Protein/Milks,
1 Fat, 40 Bonus
Calories.

Per serving:
310 Calories,
7 g Total Fat,
1 g Saturated Fat,
70 mg Cholesterol,
318 mg Sodium,
13 g Total
Carbohydrate,
0 g Dietary Fiber,
46 g Protein,
107 mg Calcium.

Points per serving: 7.

1. To prepare the marinade, in a gallon-size sealable plastic bag, combine the honey, soy sauce, lemon juice, oil, garlic, ginger, mustard, pepper flakes and black pepper; add the halibut. Seal the bag, squeezing out the air; turn to coat the fish. Refrigerate 1 hour, turning the bag occasionally.

2. Spray the broiler or grill rack with non-stick cooking spray; set aside. Preheat the broiler or grill.

3. Drain the marinade into a small saucepan and bring to a rolling boil for 1 minute, stirring constantly. Remove from the heat.

4. Grill the fish, 5" from the heat, turning once and brushing with the marinade, until the fish flakes easily when tested with a fork, 8–10 minutes.

Grilled Garlic Shrimp

one pot

make ahead

spicy

Serving provides:
2 Protein/Milks,
1 Fat.

Per serving:
161 Calories,
4 g Total Fat,
1 g Saturated Fat,
172 mg Cholesterol,
178 mg Sodium,
5 g Total Carbohy-
drate, 1 g Dietary
Fiber, 24 g Protein,
80 mg Calcium.

Points per serving: 3.

(See photo insert.)

These absolutely delicious shrimp make great party appetizers for eight or a tasty entrée for four. Serve them over rice or toss them with pasta; they're equally good cold.

¾ pound large shrimp, peeled (leaving the tails on) and deveined

1 tablespoon rice vinegar

2 teaspoons peanut oil

3 garlic cloves, minced

¼ teaspoon hot chili paste*

1 cup trimmed snow peas, steamed

1. To "butterfly" the shrimp, slice the shrimp down the back, almost but not quite in half lengthwise.

2. To prepare the marinade, in a gallon-size sealable plastic bag, combine the vinegar, oil, garlic and chili paste; add the shrimp. Seal the bag, squeezing out the air; turn to coat the shrimp. Refrigerate about 30 minutes. Drain the shrimp, discarding the marinade.

3. Spray the broiler or grill rack with non-stick cooking spray; set aside. Preheat the broiler or grill.

4. If using wooden skewers, soak eight 10–12" skewers in enough water to cover for about 15 minutes (to prevent burning).

5. Thread the shrimp and snow peas onto the skewers in an alternating pattern. Grill the skewers, 5" from the heat, turning occasionally, until the shrimp are barely opaque, 2–3 minutes.

---

*See Glossary, page 133.

Grilled Jade Scallops

makes 4 servings

Throughout China, jade is so treasured that dishes are sometimes concocted to have a green coloring to make them extra special. Here, spinach and chives provide the green.

1 teaspoon grated lemon zest

4 tablespoons fresh lemon juice

2 tablespoons minced chives

½ teaspoon minced peeled gingerroot

1¼ pounds scallops

One 10-ounce bag spinach

1 red bell pepper, seeded and cut into 1" pieces

2 teaspoons peanut oil

1. To prepare the marinade, in a gallon-size sealable plastic bag, combine the lemon zest, 2 tablespoons of the lemon juice, 1 tablespoon of the chives and the ginger; add the scallops. Seal the bag, squeezing out the air; turn to coat the scallops. Refrigerate about 30 minutes. Drain the scallops, discarding the marinade.

2. Spray the broiler or grill rack with non-stick cooking spray; set aside. Preheat the broiler or grill.

3. If using wooden skewers, soak eight 10–12" skewers in enough water to cover for about 15 minutes (to prevent burning).

4. Wash the spinach leaves thoroughly, but do not dry them. Place the spinach leaves in a large saucepan; cook with only the water that clings to them, stirring as needed, 2–3 minutes, until just wilted. Transfer to a serving bowl.

5. Thread the scallops and pepper evenly onto the skewers in an alternating pattern. Brush all over with 1 teaspoon of the oil. Grill the skewers, 5" from the heat, turning occasionally, until the scallops are barely opaque, 2–3 minutes.

6. Remove the scallops and pepper from the skewers and combine with the spinach. Sprinkle with the remaining 1 tablespoon of the lemon juice, 1 tablespoon of the chives and 1 teaspoon of the oil; toss to combine. Serve at once.

one pot

Serving provides:
2 Fruit/Vegetables,
2 Protein/Milks,
1 Fat.

Per serving:
180 Calories,
4 g Total Fat,
1 g Saturated Fat,
47 mg Cholesterol,
318 mg Sodium,
10 g Total Carbohydrate,
3 g Dietary Fiber,
27 g Protein,
150 mg Calcium.

Points per serving: 3.

Barbecued Tofu Kebabs

makes 4 servings

make ahead

spicy

vegetarian

Serving provides:
1 Fruit/Vegetable,
1 Protein/Milk, 1 Fat.

Per serving:
126 Calories,
6 g Total Fat,
1 g Saturated Fat,
0 mg Cholesterol,
483 mg Sodium,
11 g Total
Carbohydrate,
3 g Dietary Fiber,
8 g Protein,
67 mg Calcium.

Points per serving: 2.

These tasty kebabs will convert anyone who thinks tofu is bland and mushy. Prepare the tofu a day ahead to press out some of its water (making it firmer), and to allow the tofu to marinate and absorb the flavors fully.

¾ pound reduced-fat firm tofu

2 tablespoons reduced-sodium
   soy sauce

4 teaspoons peanut oil

1 tablespoon rice vinegar

1 tablespoon hoisin sauce

2 garlic cloves, minced

½ teaspoon hot chili paste*

2 cups broccoli florets, steamed

1 red bell pepper, seeded and cut into
   1½" pieces

1. To press the tofu, place it between 2 flat plates. Weight the top plate with a heavy object (try a heavy can or a cast-iron skillet), until the tofu bulges at the sides but does not split. Let stand about 30 minutes, then pour off the water that has accumulated. Cut the tofu into 1½" cubes.

2. To prepare the marinade, in a gallon-size sealable plastic bag, combine the soy sauce, oil, vinegar, hoisin sauce, garlic and chili paste; add the tofu. Seal the bag, squeezing out the air; turn to coat the tofu. Refrigerate at least 24 hours, turning the bag occasionally. Drain the tofu, reserving the marinade.

3. Spray the broiler or grill rack with non-stick cooking spray; set aside. Preheat the broiler or grill.

4. If using wooden skewers, soak eight 10–12" skewers in enough water to cover for about 15 minutes (to prevent burning).

5. Thread the tofu, broccoli and pepper evenly onto the skewers in an alternating pattern. Brush all over with the reserved marinade. Grill the skewers, 5" from the heat, turning occasionally, until the tofu is browned, 8–10 minutes.

See Glossary, page 133.

Soy, Sensibly

For centuries, the Chinese have been eating soy foods, averaging about 20 grams daily of soy protein (by contrast, Americans get less than 5 grams per day). Evidence is building that this soy-rich diet may help protect the Chinese from some of the "diseases of affluence" that are prominent in Western countries, like heart disease and certain types of cancers.

One important study showed that people who substituted soy protein for some or all of the animal protein in their diets were able to lower their cholesterol significantly. Other studies suggest that people who eat just one serving of a soy food per day (say, a half cup of tofu or one cup of soy milk) have lower incidences of breast, colon, lung and prostate cancers.

Soybeans are rich in isoflavones, estrogen-like compounds that may slow estrogen production in premenopausal women, possibly helping to lower breast-cancer risk. (Paradoxically, because isoflavones resemble estrogen, they may help relieve hot flashes and other symptoms of estrogen withdrawal during menopause—and possibly help prevent osteoporosis.) Soybeans also contain phytic acid—an antioxidant and a likely cancer fighter.

With all these possible benefits, it makes sense to try to eat a serving or two of soy foods daily—easy to do if you're a Chinese-food fan. Good soy sources include tofu, soy milk, miso (fermented soybean paste) or tempeh (slabs of fermented soybeans), cellophane noodles, and fresh or frozen soybeans (available in health-food stores). Soy sauce, alas, doesn't contain the health-boosting compounds.

You'll also find soy in some nondairy cheeses, meat substitutes like soy burgers or Textured Vegetable Protein (TVP), and nondairy frozen desserts—but many of these can be high in fat. Read the labels and choose low-fat versions of these products whenever possible.

Stuffed Tofu Packets

make ahead

spicy

vegetarian

Serving provides:
2 Protein/Milks,
1 Fat.

Per serving:
120 Calories,
7 g Total Fat,
1 g Saturated Fat,
0 mg Cholesterol,
266 mg Sodium,
5 g Total Carbohy-
drate, 1 g Dietary
Fiber, 9 g Protein,
51 mg Calcium.

Points per serving: 3.

These pretty little packets have a lot of flavor. In China, they're often stuffed with ground pork; here, flavored greens and peanuts make a satisfying substitute.

1 pound firm reduced-fat tofu, cut into 2 squares

3 tablespoons rice vinegar

1 teaspoon Asian sesame oil

One ½" piece peeled gingerroot, minced

¼ teaspoon salt

1 teaspoon peanut oil

½ red bell pepper, seeded and diced

1 scallion, finely minced

1 garlic clove, finely minced

½ cup finely chopped bok choy greens

¼ cup unsalted dry-roasted peanuts, coarsely chopped

1 teaspoon hoisin sauce

¼ teaspoon hot chili paste*

1. To press the tofu, place it between 2 flat plates. Weight the top plate with a heavy object (try a heavy can or a cast-iron skillet), until the tofu bulges at the sides but does not split. Let stand about 30 minutes, then pour off the water that has accumulated.

2. To prepare the marinade, in a gallon-size sealable plastic bag, combine the vinegar, sesame oil, ginger and salt; add the tofu. Seal the bag, squeezing out the air; turn to coat the tofu. Refrigerate at least 24 hours, turning the bag occasionally. Drain the tofu, discarding the marinade.

3. Spray the broiler or grill rack with non-stick cooking spray; set aside. Preheat the broiler or grill. Cut eight 10"-square pieces of foil.

4. To prepare the filling, in a medium non-stick skillet, heat the peanut oil. Add the pepper, scallion and garlic; cook, stirring as needed, about 1 minute. Stir in the bok choy and cook until wilted, about 1 minute. Stir in the peanuts, hoisin sauce and chili paste; cook until heated through, about 1 minute. Remove from the heat.

5. Cut both of the tofu squares into quarters on the diagonal to make 4 triangles. Set each triangle upright on its longest side. With a small knife, cut a small pocket into the top of each triangle, removing about 1 teaspoon of the tofu. Finely chop the removed tofu and stir it into the greens mixture. Stuff each pocket with the greens-tofu mixture. Wrap each tofu triangle in a foil square. Grill, 5" from the heat, until piping hot, 8–10 minutes; serve at once.

*See Glossary, page 133.

Spicy Grilled Tofu

make ahead

spicy

vegetarian

Serving provides:
2 Protein/Milks,
1 Fat, 50 Bonus
Calories.

Per serving:
157 Calories,
7 g Total Fat,
1 g Saturated Fat,
0 mg Cholesterol,
699 mg Sodium,
14 g Total
Carbohydrate,
0 g Dietary Fiber,
8 g Protein,
86 mg Calcium.

Points per serving: 4.

Reduced-fat tofu is available in some supermarkets and most natural food stores.

1 pound firm reduced-fat tofu

¼ cup reduced-sodium soy sauce

3 tablespoons firmly packed dark
    brown sugar

4 teaspoons sesame seeds

4 teaspoons Asian sesame oil

1 tablespoon minced cilantro

3 garlic cloves, minced

¼ teaspoon cayenne

¼ teaspoon ground ginger

1. To press the tofu, place it between 2 flat plates. Weight the top plate with a heavy object (try a heavy can or a cast-iron skillet), until the tofu bulges at the sides but does not split. Let stand about 30 minutes, then pour off the water that has accumulated. Cut the tofu into 12 equal pieces.

2. To prepare the marinade, in a gallon-size sealable plastic bag, combine the soy sauce, brown sugar, sesame seeds, oil, cilantro, garlic, cayenne and ginger; add the tofu. Seal the bag, squeezing out the air; turn to coat the tofu. Marinate at room temperature, turning occasionally, 2 hours.

3. Spray the grill rack with nonstick cooking spray; set aside. Preheat the grill.

4. Drain the marinade into a small saucepan and place on the grill to heat. Thread 3 pieces of tofu onto each of 4 metal skewers; grill, 5" from the heat, turning once, about 10 minutes. Top each skewer evenly with the marinade.

Smoky Grilled Eggplant

makes 4 servings

rush hour

spicy

vegetarian

Serving provides:
1 Fruit/Vegetable,
1 Fat.

Per serving:
90 Calories,
5 g Total Fat,
1 g Saturated Fat,
0 mg Cholesterol,
179 mg Sodium,
12 g Total
Carbohydrate,
2 g Dietary Fiber,
2 g Protein,
52 mg Calcium.

Points per serving: 2.

When grilled, eggplant develops a smoky flavor and chewy texture, making it a wonderful meat substitute. Combined with this complex, sweet-sour dressing, it's an irresistible side dish or sandwich filling. If you find tender baby eggplants in your market, slice them lengthwise rather than in rounds.

3 tablespoons rice vinegar

1 tablespoon peanut oil

1 teaspoon Asian sesame oil

¼ teaspoon hot chili paste*

1 medium (1¼-pound) eggplant, cut into ¼" slices

1 tablespoon reduced-sodium soy sauce

2 teaspoons sugar

1 teaspoon hot Chinese mustard

1. Spray the broiler or grill rack with non-stick cooking spray; set aside. Preheat the broiler or grill.

2. In a gallon-size sealable plastic bag, combine 1 tablespoon of the vinegar, the peanut oil, sesame oil and chili paste; add the eggplant slices. Seal the bag and shake several times to coat the slices.

3. Grill the slices in batches, 5" from the heat, turning once, until softened, 4–5 minutes. Transfer to a serving bowl.

4. In a small bowl, whisk together the remaining 2 tablespoons of the vinegar, the soy sauce, sugar and mustard; drizzle over the eggplant slices and toss. Let stand about 10 minutes at room temperature to blend flavors.

*See Glossary, page 133.

Sesame-Grilled Mushrooms

makes 4 servings

one pot

rush hour

vegetarian

Serving provides:
1 Fruit/Vegetable,
1 Fat.

Per serving:
47 Calories,
3 g Total Fat,
0 g Saturated Fat,
0 mg Cholesterol,
154 mg Sodium,
5 g Total Carbohy-
drate, 1 g Dietary
Fiber, 2 g Protein,
6 mg Calcium.

Points per serving: 1.

With their subtle sesame flavor, these mushrooms make a fabulous side dish, and the skewers are easy to slide onto the sides of the grill as you're cooking the main dish. Try them sliced into a salad or on a sandwich.

1 tablespoon reduced-sodium soy sauce

2 teaspoons Asian sesame oil

1 teaspoon rice vinegar

12 large mushrooms

1. Spray the broiler or grill rack with non-stick cooking spray; set aside. Preheat the broiler or grill.

2. If using wooden skewers, soak four 10–12" skewers in enough water to cover for about 15 minutes (to prevent burning).

3. In a small bowl, whisk the soy sauce, oil and vinegar.

4. Thread the mushrooms onto the skewers; brush on all sides with the soy sauce mixture. Grill the mushrooms, 5" from the heat, turning occasionally, until browned on all sides, 4–5 minutes; serve at once.

Grilled Tomatoes with Chinese Pesto

makes 4 servings

one pot

rush hour

vegetarian

Serving provides:
1 Fruit/Vegetable,
1 Fat.

Per serving:
99 Calories,
6 g Total Fat,
1 g Saturated Fat,
0 mg Cholesterol,
166 mg Sodium,
11 g Total
Carbohydrate,
2 g Dietary Fiber,
2 g Protein,
18 mg Calcium.

Points per serving: 2.

This pretty, unusually flavored dish is great with barbecue. If you prefer, prepare it with 8 plum tomatoes and serve them as appetizers.

3 tablespoons minced cilantro

2 scallions, thinly sliced

2 tablespoons walnuts, toasted* and
  finely chopped

1 tablespoon reduced-sodium soy sauce

2 teaspoons peanut oil

1 teaspoon Asian sesame oil

1 garlic clove, minced

4 tomatoes, halved horizontally

2 teaspoons firmly packed dark
  brown sugar

1. Spray the broiler or grill rack with non-stick cooking spray; set aside. Preheat the broiler or grill.

2. To prepare the pesto, in a small bowl, combine the cilantro, scallions, walnuts, soy sauce, 1 teaspoon of the peanut oil, the sesame oil and garlic.

3. Brush the tomatoes with the remaining 1 teaspoon of the peanut oil; sprinkle the cut sides evenly with the brown sugar. Grill the tomatoes, cut-side down, until lightly browned, 2–3 minutes; turn over and cook until soft but not falling apart, 1–2 minutes. Transfer to a plate.

4. With a small spoon, spread 2 teaspoons of the pesto mixture over the cut side of each tomato half; serve at once.

---

*To toast the walnuts, preheat the oven to 350° F. Spread the walnuts in a shallow baking pan; bake, stirring as needed, until golden brown, 8–10 minutes.

GLOSSARY

Cellophane Noodles   Also called bean threads, these thin, translucent noodles are made from the starch of green mung beans. Sold dried in Asian markets and some supermarkets, they can be tossed into soups or, after reconstituting in warm water, in stir-fried and noodle dishes.

Chili Oil   Made by steeping red chile peppers in vegetable oil, this spicy-hot red oil is widely used in Chinese cooking. Find it in Asian markets and many supermarkets.

Chinese Broccoli   Similar to broccoli, which can be used a substitute, Chinese broccoli is available in Asian markets.

Chinese Sausage   This dried sausage, readily available at Asian butcher shops, has a somewhat sweet flavor. Substitute pepperoni, chorizo, smoked turkey or ham if you prefer.

Daikon Radish   This crisp, juicy, white radish has a mild flavor with a tangy bite. Often used raw in salads or shredded as a garnish, it adds crunch to stir-fried dishes. Ranging from 6 to 15 inches in length, with white or black smooth skin, it is usually cucumber- or football-shaped. Refrigerated in a plastic bag, it will keep up to one week. Look for it in Asian markets and some natural food stores.

Dried Chinese Black Mushroom Caps   Made from dried shiitake mushroom caps (always remove the stems), these essential ingredients in the Chinese larder provide a smoky, meat-like flavor to many dishes. They can be found in Asian markets and are usually sold in varying grades. The mushrooms that are thin and broken are cheaper and generally less flavorful than the larger, thicker ones, which have a more pronounced taste. Store them in an airtight bag for up to a year; to use, reconstitute them in hot water until soft.

Dried Orange (or Tangerine) Rind   Primarily used as a seasoning, dried citrus rinds contribute a deep citrus flavor to many dishes. They will keep indefinitely in a tightly covered jar. Find them in Asian markets, or make your own by drying the rinds in the sun until they are completely hardened.

Dried Szechuan Chile Peppers   These slim, fiery-hot red chiles are indispensable in many Szechuan dishes. Their tiny yellow seeds are the hottest part; cutting off the tip of a pepper and shaking out its seeds tames its heat considerably—but they're still plenty potent. Leave them whole—it's traditional, and the whole peppers are easier to avoid when you're eating. Store them in an airtight plastic bag for up to a year. Szechuan chile peppers can be found in Asian markets and some gourmet grocery stores. If unavailable, substitute with a small amount of crushed red pepper flakes.

Fermented Black Beans   These are black beans that have been preserved in brine and dried. Their briny flavor is quite delicate, and they are often used in seafood and vegetable mixtures. Find fermented black beans in Asian markets, where they are usually quite inexpensive. Store them in an airtight plastic bag in the refrigerator; they'll keep for up to a year.

Fideos   These very thin, vermicelli-like noodles are available in most supermarkets.

Five-Spice Powder   An aromatic mixture that usually includes ground cinnamon, cloves, fennel seed, nutmeg, star anise and/or Szechuan peppercorns. In Szechuan cooking, it is often used in marinades and as a dipping powder for fried foods. Find it in Asian markets and gourmet grocery stores.

Hot Chili Paste   Made from mashed red-hot chile peppers, vinegar and seasonings (often including garlic), this pungent condiment adds fiery zest to many dishes. Stored in the refrigerator, it will keep for over a year, but its potency decreases as it ages. Find it in Asian markets and gourmet grocery stores; if unavailable, substitute with crushed red pepper flakes.

Oyster Sauce   A rich, deeply flavored cured condiment made from oysters, salt, soy sauce and other seasonings. It is often used in Cantonese-style fish dishes. Found in many supermarkets and Asian markets, it is well worth its price; just a little adds a lot of complex flavor to many dishes, and it keeps indefinitely in the refrigerator.

Star Anise   This hard seed pod of a Chinese evergreen tree looks like a nut-brown, eight-pointed star with a pea-size seed in each of its segments. Its licorice-like flavor is similar to anise seed and can be used interchangeably with that spice. It can be found in Asian markets and some supermarkets.

Sticky Rice   This short-grain rice with a glutinous texture is available in Asian markets and some natural food stores.

Szechuan Peppercorns   These reddish-brown seeds of the prickly ash tree have a sharp, aromatic flavor. Find them in Asian markets and some gourmet grocery stores; they'll keep indefinitely in an airtight container. To use, toast them in an ungreased skillet for one minute, until they begin to smoke; then crush them in a mortar and pestle or a spice grinder. Sift out the ground shells through a fine sieve. Kept in an airtight container, the powder will keep up to six months.

Tempeh   This fermented cake is made from soybeans and sometimes other grains. High in protein and easily digestible, it has a smoky, meaty flavor and texture that make it an ideal meat substitute. Available in Asian markets and natural food stores, it will last up to one week in the refrigerator, and it freezes well.

Tree Ear Fungi   Also known as cloud ears or wood ears, these mildly flavored mushrooms grow along the sides of tree trunks. They are sold dried in Asian markets and can be reconstituted by soaking in hot water. They are most commonly used in stir-fried dishes and soups, adding a silky-firm texture. In an airtight plastic bag, they'll keep up to a year.

Wheat Gluten   This meat-like product is used often in Chinese vegetarian cooking. Made from a wheat dough that has been rinsed and kneaded until all its starch is gone, leaving only the protein (gluten) behind, it has a bland flavor yet a firm, chewy texture. It can be found fresh, canned and frozen in Asian markets, and will last up to one week in the refrigerator. Natural food stores often sell Japanese-style wheat gluten, called "seitan." If either type is unavailable, substitute with firm tofu that has been pressed in a cheesecloth-lined sieve for several hours to remove its moisture.

INDEX

Metric Conversions

If you are converting the recipes in this book to metric measurements, use the following chart as a guide.

Volume		Weight		Length		Oven Temperatures	
¼ teaspoon	1 milliliter	1 ounce	30 grams	1 inch	25 millimeters	250°F	120°C
½ teaspoon	2 milliliters	¼ pound	120 grams	1 inch	2.5 centimeters	275°F	140°C
1 teaspoon	5 milliliters	½ pound	240 grams			300°F	150°C
1 tablespoon	15 milliliters	¾ pound	360 grams			325°F	160°C
2 tablespoons	30 milliliters	1 pound	480 grams			350°F	180°C
3 tablespoons	45 milliliters					375°F	190°C
¼ cup	50 milliliters					400°F	200°C
⅓ cup	75 milliliters					425°F	220°C
½ cup	125 milliliters					450°F	230°C
⅔ cup	150 milliliters					475°F	250°C
¾ cup	175 milliliters					500°F	260°C
1 cup	250 milliliters					525°F	270°C
1 quart	1 liter						

Dry and Liquid Measurement Equivalents

Teaspoons	Tablespoons	Cups	Fluid Ounces
3 teaspoons	1 tablespoon		½ fluid ounce
6 teaspoons	2 tablespoons	⅛ cup	1 fluid ounce
8 teaspoons	2 tablespoons plus 2 teaspoons	⅙ cup	
12 teaspoons	4 tablespoons	¼ cup	2 fluid ounces
15 teaspoons	5 tablespoons	⅓ cup minus 1 teaspoon	
16 teaspoons	5 tablespoons plus 1 teaspoon	⅓ cup	
18 teaspoons	6 tablespoons	⅓ cup plus two teaspoons	3 fluid ounces
24 teaspoons	8 tablespoons	½ cup	4 fluid ounces
30 teaspoons	10 tablespoons	½ cup plus 2 tablespoons	5 fluid ounces
32 teaspoons	10 tablespoons plus 2 teaspoons	⅔ cup	
36 teaspoons	12 tablespoons	¾ cup	6 fluid ounces
42 teaspoons	14 tablespoons	1 cup plus 2 tablespoons	7 fluid ounces
45 teaspoons	15 tablespoons	1 cup minus 1 tablespoon	
48 teaspoons	16 tablespoons	1 cup	8 fluid ounces

Note: Measurement of less than ⅛ teaspoon is considered a dash or a pinch.

RD2FF